A MAN OF THE BEATITUDES

Pier Giorgio Frassati, age 16

A Man of the Beatitudes
Pier Giorgio Frassati

by

Luciana Frassati

WITH AN INTRODUCTION BY
Karl Rahner, S.J.

IGNATIUS PRESS   SAN FRANCISCO

Title of the Italian original:
Pier Giorgio Frassati: I giorni della sua vita
© 1975 Vita Nova, s.p.a.
Second edition © 1993 Edizioni Studium, Rome

Translated into English by Dinah Livingstone
© 1990 St. Paul Publications, Middlegreen Slough, England

Revised edition, adapted and edited by Patricia O'Rourke
© 2000 Novalis, Saint Paul University, Ottawa, Canada

Reprinted in 2001 Ignatius Press, San Francisco
ISBN 978-0-89870-861-5
Library of Congress control number 2001088854
Printed in the United States of America ∞

"The power of the Spirit of Truth, united to Christ, made Pier Giorgio Frassati a modern witness to the hope which springs from the Gospel and to the grace of salvation which works in human hearts. . . . By his example he proclaims that a life lived in Christ's Spirit—the Spirit of the Beatitudes—is 'blessed', and that only the person who becomes a 'man or woman of the Beatitudes' can succeed in communicating love and peace to others."

—JOHN PAUL II

HOMILY FROM THE BEATIFICATION MASS
OF BLESSED PIER GIORGIO FRASSATI,
MAY 20, 1990

CONTENTS

FOREWORD

As Catholic chaplain of the University of Toronto for the
past six years, and having worked with students and young
adults for all of my priestly ministry, I am convinced now
more than ever that the world today, and especially young
people, have increasing need of the fascinating and intriguing
lives of the saints. In beatifying Pier Giorgio Frassati, on May
20, 1990, Pope John Paul II offered to the whole Church,
and particularly to Catholic young adults at the university, a
wonderful Gospel artist—one who judged and critiqued the
world from a different set of data, information, and knowledge. Pier Giorgio's standards were found in a blueprint entitled the Beatitudes, and he attempted, in his own time and
unique ways, to take that extraordinary Gospel vision and
transpose it onto the world. G. K. Chesterton said that
"[such] people have exaggerated what the world and the
Church have forgotten." Sometimes on a university campus,
such individuals are called mad, unrealistic, dreamers. In our
Church, we call them saints.

Pier Giorgio Frassati was born in Turin, Italy, on April 6,
1901. His mother, Adelaide Ametis, was a painter. His father,
Alfredo, an agnostic, was the founder and director of the
liberal newspaper *La Stampa* and was influential in Italian
politics, holding positions as an Italian senator and ambassador to Germany. Pier Giorgio was educated at home with his
sister, Luciana (the author of this book), who was one year
younger than he, before attending with her a public school

and finally a school run by the Jesuits. There he joined the Marian Sodality and the Apostleship of Prayer and obtained permission to receive daily Communion (which was rare at that time).

He developed a deep spiritual life, which he never hesitated to share with his friends. The Eucharist and the Blessed Mother were the two poles of his world of prayer. At the age of seventeen, in 1918, he joined the St. Vincent de Paul Society and dedicated much of his spare time to serving the sick and the needy, caring for orphans, and assisting the demobilized servicemen returning from World War I. Pier Giorgio saw Jesus in the poor. When a friend asked him how he could bear to enter the dirty and smelly places where they lived, he answered: "Remember always that it is to Jesus that you go: I see a special light we do not have around the sick, the poor, the unfortunate." Like his father, he was strongly anti-Fascist and did nothing to hide his political views. He was often involved in disputes, first with anticlerical Communists and later with Fascists.

Athletic, full of life, always surrounded by friends, whom he inspired with his life, Pier Giorgio chose not to become a priest or religious, preferring to give witness to the Gospel as a lay person. Just before receiving his university degree in mining engineering, he contracted poliomyelitis, which doctors later speculated he caught from the sick for whom he cared. After six days of terrible suffering, Pier Giorgio died at the age of twenty-four on July 4, 1925. His last preoccupation on earth was for the poor. On the eve of his death, with a paralyzed hand he scribbled a message to a friend, asking him to purchase "and charge to my account" the medicine needed for injections to be given to a poor sick man he had been visiting.

Pier Giorgio's funeral was a triumph. The streets of Turin

were lined with a multitude of mourners who were unknown to his family: clergy and students, and the poor and the needy whom he had served so unselfishly for seven years. At the end of the book his sister writes of the moment: "Amid sorrow and dismay, the tears of Father Righini, the exaltation of Father Ibertis, O.P., the sobs of Signora Converso, Albertini Luigi's embrace of our father, the handkerchiefs, the rosaries, the crowds of poor people come to watch the coffin go by, I barely realized that a new message was being born."

That message has spread throughout the entire world. Last fall, for the feast of All Saints, the Newman Centre Catholic Mission at the University of Toronto, as a project for the Great Jubilee, unveiled a series of new stained-glass windows commemorating the heroes and heroines of our faith of the last century. Among the "cloud of witnesses" in the twelve new windows is Blessed Pier Giorgio Frassati. We were privileged to have present for the ceremony Pier Giorgio's niece (the daughter of the author of this book), Wanda Gawronska, who came from Rome for the dedication ceremony. In her moving testimony before an audience of hundreds of young people, Gawronska said: "God gave Pier Giorgio all the external attributes that could have led him to make the wrong choices: a wealthy family, very good looks, manhood, health, being the only heir of a powerful family. But Pier Giorgio listened to the invitation of Christ: 'Come, follow me.' He anticipated by at least fifty years the Church's understanding and new direction on the role of the laity." I myself think that Pier Giorgio Frassati is probably the first saint to have lived the encyclical *Rerum Novarum*.

In reading Luciana's moving personal story of her brother, Pier Giorgio, young adults can find in this handsome young outdoorsman someone with whom they can identify. He shared with them all the problems they experience today: the duty of study; the threatening cloud always hanging over him of final exams; involvement in political debates and election propaganda; radical decisions to be made about his life; the difficulty of keeping a daily commitment to prayer; the pain of falling madly in love; a father and mother who were struggling in their own relationship. How many young people struggle with these same things every day! Pier Giorgio's life speaks eloquently and profoundly to the contemporary reality of university pastoral ministry.

April 6, 2001, marks the one hundredth anniversary of his birth. This astonishing young man, whom Pope John Paul II has repeatedly called "the man of the eight Beatitudes", had a strong influence on this former Polish university professor, later to be Cardinal Archbishop of Krakow, and then Bishop of Rome. In beatifying only Frassati in St. Peter's Square on May 20, 1990, the Pope said in his homily:

> Certainly, at a superficial glance, Frassati's life-style, that of a modern young man who was full of life, does not present anything out of the ordinary. This, however, is the originality of his virtue, which invites us to reflect upon it and impels us to imitate it. In him faith and daily events are harmoniously fused, so that adherence to the Gospel is translated into loving care for the poor and the needy in a continual crescendo until the very last days of the sickness which led to his death. His love for beauty and art, his passion for sports and mountains, his attention to society's problems did not inhibit his constant relationship with the Absolute.
>
> By his example he proclaims that a life lived in Christ's Spirit, the Spirit of the Beatitudes, is "blessed", and that only the person who becomes a "man or woman of the Beatitudes" can succeed in communicating love and peace to others. He repeats that it is really worth giving up everything to serve the Lord. He testifies that holiness is

possible for everyone, and that only the revolution of charity can enkindle the hope of a better future in the hearts of people. He left this world rather young, but he made a mark upon our entire century, and not only on our century.

Pier Giorgio's mortal remains, found completely incorrupt upon their exhumation of March 31, 1981, were transferred from the family tomb in Pollone to the cathedral in Turin. Many pilgrims, especially students and young people, have journeyed to the tomb of the young blessed to seek favors and the courage to follow his example. Pope John Paul II would undoubtedly be thrilled to know that the Pontifical Council for the Laity has arranged that Pier Giorgio's body be brought from the Turin Cathedral to Rome to coincide with the Jubilee of Youth and the World Youth Day 2000! In the Eternal City, Frassati will be venerated by the hundreds of thousands of young people and pilgrims who will journey to Rome and find in him a Gospel artist of supreme beauty, one who was like themselves, one who lived in this world, with all of its shadows and light, all of its sadness and beauty. They will find in Pier Giorgio Frassati what Jesus' sermon on a Galilean hillside really meant.

I know that I speak on behalf of the Frassati family and the Pontifical Council for the Laity in expressing deep gratitude to the publisher and Novalis for making the age-old message of the Beatitudes come alive once again in a new and brilliant way through the life of Blessed Pier Giorgio Frassati: a model, a hero, and a Gospel artist for our times.

Fr. Thomas Rosica, C.S.B.
Executive Director and Pastor
Newman Centre Catholic Mission at the University of Toronto
May 20, 2000

INTRODUCTION

Famous writers such as Papini, La Pira, and Cardinal Lercaro have written prefaces to books about Pier Giorgio Frassati. My reason for writing a brief introduction to this biography of him is not to give the book importance, but because I am among the few living Germans who knew Frassati personally, and for fifty years I have kept a vivid memory of him. I am not going to give any personal reminiscences, which would only repeat and confirm what the book itself does better. If I may immodestly suppose that the reader will read my introduction first, I would like to use it to explain one or two things that may make it easier to read the book.

In order to appreciate the value of Frassati's life and him as a person, a few indications will be sufficient here. When I look back at the years after the First World War, with their many initiatives and movements in the world and Church at the time, and I recall the impression that Frassati made on me then (when I knew much less about him than I know now), I have to confess frankly that I thought of him as just one among many Christian young people in the Catholic youth movement at that time. There were so many of them. This impression should be understood as praise, not disparagement. Frassati represented the pure, happy, handsome Christian youth, given to prayer, enthusiastic about everything that is free and beautiful, interested in social problems, who had the Church and her fate at heart, and had a serene and manly spontaneity. Young people like this deserve all admiration, even if there are many of them—and at that time there were (but has the springtime of these marvelous promises resulted in an autumn worthy of them?). Pier Giorgio Frassati was something more. The reader will gather this from reading this modern *vita sanctorum*. Why more? Let me put it simply. Certainly at a superficial glance his inner world and style of life do not offer anything particularly original—and he was far from thinking they did! There were plenty of young Christians like him at that time, thank God, in Germany, France, and Italy.

However, I am convinced that few of them coming from the liberal environment of the high bourgeoisie became like Pier Giorgio Frassati, without this being attributable to the usual psychological mechanism of children rebelling against their parents. His uniqueness consists in the fact that this spirit of rebellion is not found in him. Frassati is a Christian, simply and in an absolutely spontaneous way, as if it were something spontaneous for everybody. He has the strength and courage to be what he is, not from opposition to his parents' generation, not from a prognosis and diagnosis of the culture of the time, or some such idea, but from the Christian reality itself: that God is, that what sustains us is prayer, that the Eucharist nourishes what is eternal in us, that all people are brothers and sisters.

We might think that his practical and unromantic character, his intelligence, which was just "normal", the solidity of the Italian family circle, would have made it a priori impossible for Pier Giorgio to be Christian in that way, although there was a revival after the First World War. Nevertheless he became a spontaneous and total Christian, a church-going Catholic, without therefore saying "Amen" to all ecclesiastical traditions, full of apostolic zeal, always ready to help his neighbor in a practical way. None of this is explained either by his family situation (as the book very clearly shows) or the cultural and religious situation of the time (in spite of men like Sonnenschein, Don Sturzo, and others). Here we perceive in a mysterious way that God's grace is not something predictable. Here suddenly is a Christian in an environment that makes us think such a phenomenon belongs to the past. Here he is, happy, without being someone who goes off and tries at all costs to become different. He becomes—what a fine symbol!—the means of reconciliation for what is contradictory in his parents' lives. Is it an exaggeration for me to think that even at that time such young people were rare?

I want briefly to mention something else. At that time we were all interested in social problems; it was natural. But this social work, love for the poor, and responsibility in facing the wretchedness of others were (or became) so genuine and deep, so charged with the spirit of sacrifice in Pier Giorgio as to make him an exception among the many Christian young people of the time. At that time, many, thank God, did their bit through the Conferences of St. Vincent. But there must have been few who, while suffering the torments of death by poliomyelitis, would still feel it their duty to think of the poor.

Here, as in other circumstances, the reader will easily guess, Pier Giorgio's life is so rich, so serene, so almost thoughtlessly cheerful (in spite of all the family problems): riding, skiing, reading Dante and other poets, in the company of friends and girls, singing, having ardent political discussions, clashing with the police, and doing so many other things characteristic of the golden youth. (He described all these with enthusiasm while he was showing us photos.) But in him all of it suddenly acquires a depth and seriousness deriving from the absolute supremacy of the Christian faith in God and eternal life, which cannot fail to strike the reader.

God does not grant to all the grace to die young, when everything is morning promise and immaculate beginning. And not every early death is the fulfillment of this beginning. But here the immaculate beginning was accepted, and the threat or rather the promise of the Lord's Cross embraced willingly in death. But we should not think of this life only in terms of that transfiguring melancholy conferred by the premature death of the young. For all that we know, we do not want to be his judges. Here we have someone who lived his Christianity with a naturalness that is almost awe-inspiring, surprisingly unproblematic and inviting. In fact, his problems, often bathed in silent tears, were immersed in the grace of his faith: in prayer, in Holy Communion (the Bread of life and death), and in loving his neighbor. It should not irritate us that when he tried to express what was in him he began stammering phrases from traditional piety. Even such words, if taken rightly, become fresh.

Half a century later, so many things have changed. But here, in spite of the inevitable style of the time, is simply a young Christian life. This book describing a life that attained holiness many years ago deserves to be read today and meditated on. There are many Christians, and there are also many who, with God's grace, have lived and borne witness to their faith in a heroic way. But we can never have enough of these examples. None of them is a natural phenomenon, but rather each is always a miracle of divine grace. If the reader reads this book in the right spirit, he will meet a heroic Christian. Now let him praise the divine grace and pray that Pier Giorgio Frassati intercedes with God for himself and for us all.

Karl Rahner

Author's Note

On October 1, 1921, Pier Giorgio—introduced by the famous pastor Karl Sonnenschein, his old special friend called the St. Francis of Berlin—became a guest of the Rahner family, which included Karl and Hugo among its seven children. My brother spent "unforgettable days" with them. This was partly because of the affection and understanding he received from Louise Rahner. At the time she was celebrating her silver wedding anniversary. She was immediately attracted to Pier Giorgio and his simplicity, in spite of his being an ambassador's son.

Biographers of Karl Rahner, who joined the Society of Jesus in 1922, begin their story of the great theologian's life with these words: "He was profoundly impressed by a young Italian university student, three years his senior, who died in 1925 of acute poliomyelitis in the odor of sanctity: Pier Giorgio Frassati, a Dominican tertiary, fervent daily communicant, apostle in the student world in the struggle against the old sectarian, anticlerical system and against incipient Fascism, overflowing with tireless charity toward the poor" (Charles Muller and Herbert Vorgrimler, *Karl Rahner, Théologiens et contemporains spirituels*, vol. 2 [Paris: Fleurus, 1965]).

CHAPTER 1

Beginnings

My brother, Pier Giorgio Frassati, was born in Turin on Holy Saturday, April 6, 1901, seventeen months before my entry into the world. Our family was rich and influential, but Pier Giorgio grew up to become a fierce defender of the poor, sick, and disadvantaged. A university student active in sports, and an energetic political protester, his private life was one of sacrifice and of deep devotion to Christ in the sacraments. He was beatified by Pope John Paul II on May 20, 1990. His short life (he died of poliomyelitis in 1925) was dedicated to challenging an Italian society in the midst of social turmoil.

Our father was Alfredo Frassati, the well-known founder, editor-in-chief, and owner of Turin's most important daily paper, *La Stampa,* the youngest senator, and later ambassador to Germany in 1921. Our mother, Adelaide Ametis, did many things, but her greatest joy was painting. Neither of our parents was devoutly Catholic: our father was agnostic and our mother was not deeply religious. Our mother and her sister Elena would not have missed Mass, but they were never seen by us to go to Communion or to kneel and say a prayer. The deeply religious person, in her own way, was our grandmother Linda Ametis. Her devotion to praying for the dead influenced Pier Giorgio, who, traveling to Germany at the age of twenty, took care to have an anniversary Mass said for an aunt who had died before he was born and for our great-grandmother Antonia.   *Influence*

* * *

Even at a very young age Pier Giorgio responded immediately to the needs of the weak. One day, seeing a frail woman who had knocked at the door with a barefoot child in her arms, he quickly took off his shoes and socks and gave them to her, then rapidly shut the door before anyone in the house came to protest. In the nursery school that Pier Giorgio was visiting with Grandfather, the children had lunch at midday. Pier Giorgio was intent on admiring the long marble tables with holes for the dishes, which were new to him, when at the other end of the room he saw a child in isolation because of a severe skin disorder. He went up to him and, before Sister Celeste, busy talking to Grandfather Francesco, had noticed, shared his soup, wiping out the misery on the small, lonely face.

In the evenings, Pier Giorgio often gathered wild flowers to take to his great-grandmother Antonia, who enjoyed these affectionate gifts from the little boy. Flowers were an occasion of joy but also homage to God's house. One day he met a lay worker in the garden. She had come from the nursery to pick a bunch of flowers for the chapel. Pier Giorgio ran up to her with a beautiful scarlet rose in his hand and said, "Sister . . ." "I am not a sister", replied the lay worker, but he continued imperturbably: "Sister, take this rose to Jesus for me." Surprised at the child's look, she thanked him with a phrase that sounds prophetic today: "You'll see that one day Jesus will make you a saint."

* * *

Our childhood lives were strictly controlled and isolated. The memory of those far-off days still hurts because we lacked a mother's tenderness. Our childhood was painful: the

The Frassati family villa, Pollone

days at Pollone, which was my mother's family home, or in
the Turin house where we spent our winters, were days
during which we were unable to get away from the same
faces, the same rooms, and the monotonous streets. We were
not allowed to walk about the city, stand in front of windows, give way to little stirrings of curiosity. We had to walk
briskly, without turning our heads. Our father spent those
years and many others engrossed in *La Stampa*, a refuge that
deprived the family day after day of his presence. *La Stampa*
represented my father's glory, his private kingdom away from
the Pollone household, which was the domain of my
mother's family.

The emptiness created by a sea of prohibitions forced us to
spend much time in each other's company. We learned en-
durance, the habit of discipline and obedience, and acceptance of continual sacrifices. Conversation with grown-ups

was nonexistent and forbidden. Being considered nothing or, worse, troublemakers, tempered our pride. We even suffered real hunger, presumably for the benefit of our health. However, we were capable of facing obstacles and pain with courage. At least our father, even though he rarely entered our private world, shared in our games.

* * *

Pier Giorgio grew up to be serious, fair-minded, and very good looking, with big black eyes whose whites were almost blue. He was the picture of health. He loved mountain-climbing and, on long climbs, never complained of hunger, thirst, or fatigue. He learned from our mother to resist everything that might seem like weakness or surrender. Our mother even took him on a ten-hour climb up a 10,906-foot mountain. Pier Giorgio had no special training for these excursions, although he had hiked over the Turin hills with his uncle.

* * *

In 1909 we suffered our first loss, when our much-loved grandfather, Francesco Ametis, died. We also had to abandon friends when we were sent to a different school. Even at this time, religion remained obscure to us as we had received superficial instruction from several priests. Pier Giorgio had to insist that one of our Latin instructors, Don Cojazzi, a Venetian Salesian, tell him the story of Jesus' life. He wanted to hear the words of the Gospel.

The eucharistic Christ was his sovereign Lord, whom he never ceased to adore.

* * *

By the time he was eleven, Pier Giorgio had become more and more aware of poverty. He tried to overcome it with little labors, such as collecting silver paper, tram tickets, and stamps for missionaries. He continually renounced those

Pier Giorgio with his father, 1913

*Luciana and Pier Giorgio with their father
in the offices of* La Stampa

small pleasures which are everything in childhood. He gave away the small gifts of money he received from his uncle Pietro. One day, he poured his modest fortune into his old nurse's hands because he had heard her talking about her many children and consequent deprivations.

Pier Giorgio was also, even at this early age, brave. One day, while skating, an unknown girl suddenly found herself on the edge of a dangerous hole in the ice. Pier Giorgio immediately stretched out his hand to her so that she could jump to safety. He fell in the water with a loud splash. Pier Giorgio was constantly aware of the needs of others. Our mother wrote this small note for his biography:

Alfredo was in the hall when a poor man—or rather a workman—rang the doorbell. He said he was starving and out of work. My husband sent him away because he had a nauseating smell of alcohol. Pier Giorgio was there and ran to me in tears (I was on the telephone) crying: "Mama, there is a poor man who is hungry and Papa did not give him anything to eat!" He sobbed and pulled my dress. To calm him down I said: "Run into the street and tell him to come in. We'll give him something to eat." And so he did. The child was happy. Meanwhile we asked the address of the poor workman and sent him away *without* giving him money, but with the promise to Pier Giorgio that in two hours, when we had got some information, he would be helped. Of course it was a false address and the man one of the usual deceivers and con men.

* * *

In 1912, one of our mother's paintings was bought by the king of Italy, Victor Emmanuel III. The following year our father's good work was rewarded with a seat in the Senate. Our family had become successful, though this did not affect our simplicity. It laid, however, a new burden on Pier Giorgio as he grew older. His companions mocked him for being "the senator's son".

In spite of the burdens of office, our father, in his brief free time after meals, continued to be our companion at games. Then the house came alive as we raced about. At these times, we were able to treat our father as a contemporary, addressing him by titles unworthy of his dignified position.

He asked only a little from his children: "Love each other! Do not play cards. Study." He also told us to go back to our grandmother's house in Pollone as soon as possible. We followed this advice so literally that we started regularly to go there, not only at Easter but also at Christmas, when the house was freezing. The whole visit would have been freezing if the gardener had not distracted us with games and mountain walks. Pier Giorgio had become the gardener's right hand and chose a piece of land for himself on which to grow his own vegetables and sweet peas. He hoed, he carried flower pots, honeycombs, and bundles of wood, and he refilled cans. He halved the gardener's work.

CHAPTER 2

The Jesuit School

As a child, Pier Giorgio found learning to write a nightmare. He could not easily write what he did not feel. One letter from that period shows how free and expressive his writing could be when his heart was in it:

August 14, 1907

Dear Papalino,
On this your birthday I am writing to send you lots of good wishes for your good health. I will pray to Jesus for you and I promise you to be good and to study to make up to you for all your work and the sacrifices you are making for me. Happy birthday and lots of good wishes from your

Pier Giorgio

December 19, 1907

Dear Mammina,
I love you and I am very pleased to write you this letter to send you my good wishes for your feast day. Here is a present for you of a basket made by Luciana and me.

In spite of continuous heroic efforts, the cry "You can't write" became a nagging refrain and a source of continual humiliation. Both Pier Giorgio and I failed the public examinations in 1908, but the family was more concerned with Pier Giorgio's future. As a girl, I was not expected to earn my living. In our father's mind, Pier Giorgio was already the

future director of *La Stampa*. Our mother wrote to her sister
that she feared for his future.

In the autumn of 1913, because he had failed in Latin, Pier
Giorgio and I were separated for the first time. He shows
how upset he was in this letter from private school:

> Dear Papa,
> I am confused and miserable and I don't know how to
> write to you. I saw how upset Mama was and I thought
> about you being upset too so much that I don't know how
> to say I am sorry. I am sorry that I have to stay behind and
> I am ashamed in front of my friends and sister who have
> got ahead of me. I hope you will believe in the sincerity
> of my resolve to study this year and try to make up for this
> as much as possible. You will see I'll try to prove my
> affection for you with facts.

The Istituto Sociale accepted him as a student, and the
Jesuits who ran it helped him to become more active in
charity and stronger in faith. Our mother was very anxious
that confession might involve Pier Giorgio being asked
"certain questions" that would involuntarily direct his mind
toward impure thoughts. If you speak to a pure man about
impurity, he begins to understand that impurity exists.
Alarmed, she went to the spiritual father Pietro Lombardi,
almost wanting to stop him hearing Pier Giorgio's confession. The good Jesuit reassured her by telling her he had a lot
of experience with boys. Pier Giorgio was invited to receive
Communion every morning. He was surprised because at
home he had heard "silly women" criticized if they went to
church every day. He had the desire for daily Communion,
and now it became acceptable because a wise priest suggested
it. Our mother was convinced that daily Communion would
become a mere habit. She was afraid that her son would
become a narrow-minded Catholic, and she opposed the

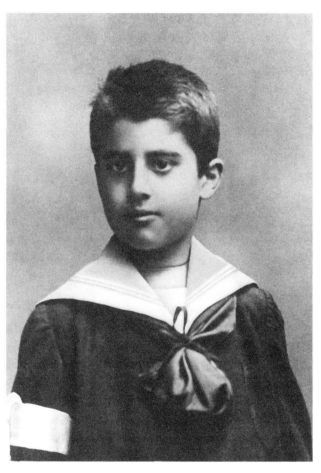

Pier Giorgio on the day of his First Communion

idea as strongly as she could. Pier Giorgio had to plead with her for four days to be allowed to accept Father Lombardi's invitation.

Pier Giorgio despised external show and refused to decorate his chest with ribbons and medals. He never agreed to become one of the officers of the Marian Sodality. However, he joined the Association of the Blessed Sacrament and the Apostleship of Prayer.[1] From then on, he always had his membership card in his pocket, as if it were his true identity card.

* * *

Although he was only thirteen, Pier Giorgio always felt the pressure of time. He was loaded with tasks, some enjoyable, some boring. Among the latter were piano lessons, which were always a torture. His usual sense of duty kept him at it for a time, then he gave it up. To these and other torments were added extremely hard studies both at school and at home.

Once the school year and secondary school admission exams were over, we took the train for Alassio, on the Riviera. There we visited Grandmother Linda Ametis. While there, Pier Giorgio had a brilliant idea. "We should grow flowers at Alassio to sell in Turin for the poor." He showed the same generosity one day when his friend Paola Marchisio pointed at a poor woman's house exclaiming: "If I were the owner of that slum I'd pull it down!" Pier Giorgio replied in distress: "Oh, Paola, if you knew how many good souls live in houses that you call slums!" For those in need, Pier Giorgio was always ready to abandon an alluring prospect, even an invitation to go on the merry-go-round at the fair. He never hesitated to explain that he had business with the poor and

[1] This association, which aims to unite the Christian life with the morning offering prayer, was founded in 1844 in France.

recorded in his notebook addresses of needy people. Our mother was worried that Pier Giorgio might become a priest, fears she communicated to Monsignor Baravalle, whom she met in the train. She told him: "Every evening at Alassio he went to Benediction in the Capuchin church nearby, while we went for a stroll with our friends, and he slipped out of the boarding house, before breakfast, to go to Mass." This was the beginning of our mother's increasing misunderstanding of her son, which continued until his death.

mother did not understand him.

CHAPTER 3

Neutralist

The year 1915 was a difficult one. As children we lost our little pleasures, from fireworks, which had the great merit of delaying bedtime, to sugar, which soon disappeared, to the usual veal, which was replaced by horsemeat. More seriously, this year was the beginning of the long-drawn-out debates between those who believed that Italy should intervene in the so-called three-months war and the neutralists who opposed intervention.

La Stampa was against immediate intervention, so, naturally, my brother and I supported this position and were proud to endure its consequences. A substitute teacher who was opposed to our father's position and who hated the name Frassati sent Pier Giorgio out of the classroom on any pretext. In vain, I tried to use my privileged position as a girl, and therefore an outsider to politics, to explain to him that my brother seemed naughty but it was only because he was the last one in the class to laugh that he got caught. But the regular teacher loved him and merely teased him by calling him "Giano Bifronte" because of his way of laughing loudly and sharing his enjoyment with friends by turning back to those sitting behind him.

The political disagreements among the pupils were more open and immediate. Their consequences were not grave, although they were often resolved with blows, like the day when Camillo Banzatti, son of the assistant director of *La*

Stampa, and Pier Giorgio were greeted by Mario Attilio Levi [a schoolmate who later became a well-known writer] with the fashionable cry: "You are traitors like your fathers!", concluding with the grievous insult "*soldini!*" [mercenaries], by which he meant we had sold ourselves for a few coins to the Central Powers.[2] Camillo, who was older and closer to Mario Attilio, took him by the scruff of the neck and gave him a few good slaps. After this "exchange of ideas", Pier Giorgio went on his way, muttering.

He was fuming, and, when it was known at home what had happened, a storm broke on his innocent shoulders. Camillo was the hero of the day while Pier Giorgio was accused of being good for nothing and was told that he would never get on in life because he had been unable to seize that magnificent occasion to strike a few blows. Pier Giorgio listened to the sermon calmly, then he looked into our mother's face and said: "We were two against one; tomorrow it will be my turn."

In spite of our neutralism, war broke out, accompanied by tears, flags in the streets, and bell ringing.

* * *

To the real tragedies of those days, a ridiculous one was added. Our mother had a vivid imagination and worried about the purity of her son:

> I had always had a terror of the crises boys are known to pass through. I have spent sleepless nights weeping and thinking about the dangers awaiting Pier Giorgio from the age of thirteen or fourteen to the age of sixteen or eighteen! I had no brothers; I never saw a boy growing up with me. So I thought: he must be with his sister.

[2] The Central Powers consisted of the triple alliance of Germany, Austria-Hungary, and Italy, which ended in World War I.

It was possible to underestimate Pier Giorgio's charity, piety, and intelligence, or to ignore his prayer life, but his purity leapt to the eye of even the least observant. It was his most "visible" virtue because it was stamped on his very being and never hidden by his humility. His purity was in-born and higher and better than ordinary modesty. It was reflected in a permanent state of reserve (also due to the fact that he had always until the age of maturity been with his sister) that did not exclude but accentuated a certain ease of manner. Accustomed, for example, to admire a nude as one admires a sunset, he learned to take an interest in the beauty of the drawing and nothing else.

The family always underestimated him. This did not make success easy for him. Our mother's worries finally cast a shadow over him, from which only death released him. Silence was the only defense against such condemnation. And this is what he practiced every day at the family table. In silence he continued to mature in himself the graces of the Holy Communion he started receiving daily at the Istituto Sociale. The two years spent at that Jesuit school gave him something more truly his, something that no one could take from him: the strength of his faith.

CHAPTER 4

General Cadorna: The "Enemy"

During the war, Pier Giorgio made himself useful by attending agricultural courses at the Istituto Bonafous and receiving a diploma. The exam consisted of cutting corn, tying it into sheaves, and storing it in the barn. Because he could ride, he was given the job of managing work in the field. In the evenings he came home proudly with a big parcel of lettuce under his arm, unless he had surrendered this small privilege to a more needy companion.

If it had not been for the war, everything would have been calm. For example, Pier Giorgio enjoyed the fifty-mile bicycle rides he made from Pollone to Turin with his friend Bellingeri. After such an exhausting trip, instead of jumping in the bath or lying down, he used to pace up and down declaiming Dante.

The bicycle was his delight, but on the day it was stolen he did not show any resentment. Our father's friend Crescentino Rampone remembers that he merely looked at the chain torn from the stair banister in the Bellingeri house and murmured: "Perhaps it was someone who needed it more than I do." The bicycle came from our hard-earned savings, from the little gifts given us by our uncle and grandmother, and my "withdrawals" from the paternal purse—a game in which, with my father's knowledge, I infiltrated his pocket with my hand, and he vainly tried to catch me.

37

Pier Giorgio always behaved the same to everyone, ruling out immediately any distinctions. He treated children lovingly. His friend Lorenzo Brinatti remembers him giving away everything in his pockets to the little refugees brought together in the D'Azeglio school gymnasium. He caressed them tenderly, acutely aware that they were orphans. He freely sent what little money he had to soldiers, and, when he met one at home, he never felt he had given enough. He said: "Now you are going to the front, and you've got no money: what's to be done? I have six lire and you can have them."

* * *

The Great War continued with its tremendous weight of sacrifice. Pier Giorgio withdrew into long silences, interrupting his reflections with agonized questions on the drama of the dead, the wounded, and the widows. He often spoke about it with Natalina Novo, the servant girl, whose brother had already been killed in the war. One day she told him the news she had heard from our father: "Two thousand mountain troops cut off from the Italian lines and shelled by enemy cannons." Dismayed, my brother asked her: "Natalina, wouldn't you give your life to stop the war?" "Certainly not," replied Natalina, "I am young, and my life is as dear to me as that of the soldiers." Pier Giorgio stared at her, saying: "I would, I would today."

Wartime politics had swept away so many old friendships: Professor Antonio Garbasso, because he was intimate with the poet Gabriele D'Annunzio, an interventionist. Another was lost because he knew and respected General Luigi Cadorna, to whom even Pier Giorgio was opposed. Another old friend was lost because he was linked to the interventionist *Corriere della Sera*. So many friends were lost. But there was a new recruit, the honorable Mario Chiaraviglio, M.P., son-in-law of Giovanni Giolitti, who confessed he had been a Freemason but insisted on reassuring our mother that he no longer belonged to any lodge: "Never mind, never mind, the stamp remains", she replied firmly. As a good deputy he gave the impression of loving words more than deeds, but at that time one theme predominated: the war, the useless killings, the over-hasty intervention, General Cadorna's disgraceful communiqué blaming the army, and not himself, for the Italian defeat at Caporetto.

We had by this time moved to a new house. Pier Giorgio became ill with chicken pox. He was not a difficult invalid but was patience and goodness personified, happy to make sacrifices so as not to disturb anyone. He remained thirsty throughout a whole night and so could not sleep. He remained quiet, justifying this by saying: "You were asleep, Mama, and I did not want to wake you." He kept up this extreme charity till the end.

As soon as we entered secondary school, we were given greater freedom. This increased our sense of responsibility, which, unconsciously, made us the center around which family life revolved. However, while our mother increasingly appreciated me, conversation between Pier Giorgio and Father remained meager. Our father often humiliated Pier Giorgio and never missed an occasion to make him understand how annoyed he was that I was not a boy and therefore would not work at *La Stampa*.

Branding him a simpleton, our father experienced the mysterious bafflement the man of the world feels when confronted with unworldliness. On the whole, in spite of his remarks, he respected his son even though he had to give up the hope that he would be like him. The evening he discovered him by his bed with his rosary in his hand, he did not say anything, but, later, he met the parish priest of Crocetta,

Alessandro Roccati, and expressed his disappointment: "What have you done to my son?" he asked. The elderly monsignor, with the authority derived from having baptized Pier Giorgio, replied, unruffled: "Perhaps, Senator, you would prefer him to fall asleep with some cheap novel on his night table?" "No, certainly not that!" was the swift reply.

That year my brother attended religion lessons. Pier Giorgio was the only one in that group of students who showed any enthusiasm. The others had determined to get no profit from the lessons, but the priest never had to throw a reproachful glance at Pier Giorgio or complain about his attitude. He was now sixteen and was in the habit of praying early in the morning and at day's end. One day he said to our cousins' maid: "Nerina, I will keep a place for you in Paradise." It was as if he already felt his end was near.

* * *

After the Italian defeat at Caporetto, Pier Giorgio felt himself even more impelled to help others. He and a friend delivered contributions by cart from local firms to a dinner for the war wounded in the Ospedale Mauriziano. He began to work in the garden at the Pollone family home to help the gardener's wife, who was now alone in the house. When the gardener came home on leave, he admired the work. The "miracles" were humble potatoes, but they were precious at the time.

In order to be called early Pier Giorgio had set up a rope alarm. A rope tied to the drawer of his bedside table was dropped from his bedroom window; at dawn the rope was shaken by the gardener. Once, when Pier Giorgio was sleeping heavily, the gardener had to shake the rope so much that it knocked over the table. Hearing the noise, Mother rushed in. Reassured by Pier Giorgio's "it's nothing", she advised him to "switch on the light next time" so he would not trip over things. From that day on, a new alarm system was used: the long bamboo cane that the gardener used to get nuts from the trees.

Prayer had become a steady feature of Pier Giorgio's day. One time, during that period, Pier Giorgio and I made an excursion to Mount Mucrone, a trip that required an overnight stay in a hostel. We arrived tired, but, as soon as we lay on the bunks, Pier Giorgio announced: "Now let's say the rosary." At home in Turin, the landlady heard a continual murmuring in the room below hers, which made her imagine that Pier Giorgio was studying hard.

* * *

"He was a poet in contemplating beautiful things and he reached heights in conversation which impressed," the theologian Francesco Ottino wrote about my brother. Nobody understood him in this, least of all our parents, although they did see him walking around the garden sonorously and dramatically declaiming Dante or Shakespeare. Even the simple people at Pollone realized that he sometimes spoke as if he were addressing the birds, the moon, the sky, alternating study with song. His voice, which was familiar to so many of them, became a signal for the girls going to work. "The Senator's son is sounding forth", they said.

Some thought that he was speaking Latin. Other, better educated ones recognized Dante's cantos. Some of them, from hearing him so often, ended up knowing them by heart. Some, like the Piacenza cousin, distinguished the *Paradiso* cantos, others, the psalms. The lawyer Schiapparelli said to his wife: "Pier Giorgio is beginning his preaching, who knows when he will stop? This morning he was in the villa's cupola sitting at the window. He had a big book in his hand. I don't know if he was learning his lesson out loud. All I could hear was 'God . . . stars . . . Dante.'"

This went on for years until his voice went silent, leaving a void. "The one who was always singing is dead", they said.

CHAPTER 5

1918—The Great Day

Pier Giorgio foresaw the consequences of the notorious Treaty of Versailles, which redivided the territories of the defeated Central Powers at the end of the war, and the fascinating, terrible Russian Revolution. Like many young people of the time, he felt charged with new responsibilities. He was, of course, delighted that peace had come. On November 4, 1918, the day the war ended, he rushed up the bell tower of the parish church of Pollone to announce the news. That same November 4 he wrote to his friend Carlo Bellingeri: "I am so happy that your saint's day is on the same day as the happiest day for the country."

In 1918, Pier Giorgio returned to the Jesuit school because he had failed his exams. He simultaneously finished stages two and three at the Istituto Sociale. We had become more distant from each other, were no longer children, and found it difficult to tell each other everything. A long time after his death I heard from the Rosminian Sister Celeste—one of the unforgettable sisters who gave our childhood a secure refuge—that he had suffered greatly because of his vocation. His slowly maturing ideas and his instinctive inclinations made him think of the priesthood, but he felt our mother's hostility to the idea. She had other aspirations for her son: a more conventional and glorious future at *La Stampa* or somewhere else in the world.

She conspired with Don Tito Zambelli, a Venetian refugee

mother
tried
to
stop
his
faith
(obstacle)

in Pollone, in which parish she had set up a school of singing. Because he often came to our house, mother asked him
to tell Pier Giorgio to stop saying so many rosaries, especially
at night. She felt that the rosary was reserved for the vigil of
All Saints' Day and, like everything else in the family, ought
to follow a precise routine.

"Is it true, Pier Giorgio, that when you are in your room
you pray for a long time?" asked Don Tito. My brother did
not answer, and the priest continued: "Yes, your mother told
me so. You are upsetting her, and she gets up in the night . . ."
"But I have so many prayers to say", murmured Pier Giorgio.
"And who has ordered you to?" "No one. I just have to."

Our mother and Don Tito tried to prevent Pier Giorgio
from following a course of which they disapproved. So certain were they that their "no" was considered beyond appeal
that they allowed him to return to the Jesuit Istituto Sociale.

How did Pier Giorgio react to these restrictions? He spoke
less and less. He joined the Sodality of Mary at the Sociale
and made the rosary his consolation and his weapon. Certainly at home there was no one to help him and no comfort
or encouragement in his faith. He used to make the sign of
the cross before entering the door of the dining room. One
day, when he was late for a meal, Mama commented: "There
he is, lost in his thoughts. He remembers Mass times but not
mealtimes. He is in his room."

His little room in Pollone was an unknown territory to
others. And even when they managed to get a glimpse of it,
they did not understand it. They believed that it was the
place where he was engaged in difficult and tiring study and
that was enough. It did not enter their heads to wonder
whether he had other things to do there. They never knew
that Sister Angelica once caught him absorbed in a vision of
God.

Pier Giorgio began to become important in his own way, without newspaper headlines or books being written about him. This happened without fuss because his personality impressed everyone who met him. He was undergoing a profound transformation. He was no longer the boy he had been at home.

Even Cardinal Richelmy, speaking of purity to the young men in the Sociale, mentioned Pier Giorgio. And Father Goria, head of the boarders, wrote that it was "a real spiritual joy to pray near him" and that he considered a "miracle" his way of attracting others to virtue by means of his many-sided and unique personality.

Pier Giorgio was seventeen and everyone at home wished he were different. He was now expected to make an attempt to become a part of public life. But he was completely taken up with his spiritual growth. His sensitivity was further honed. One day, when his companions were noisily passing through the door of the Sociale, he was the only one to realize that something was upsetting the monitor-custodian, Ernesto Fassone.

"What's the matter, Fassone?" he asked. Fassone's only son, who was fourteen, had died. Pier Giorgio stayed with him a while to comfort him. The following year, on the same day, while he was among the boys who were again pouring into the hall, he turned and stopped in front of the monitor-custodian. "Today is the anniversary of your son's death", murmured Pier Giorgio. "I will remember him at Communion." Fassone wept when he recalled these words. He knew him better than his family, who had no idea he paid such attention to life's sufferings.

Masses, communions, prayers, visiting the poor and the suffering: these filled Pier Giorgio's days, but he still had time to study. In spite of a certain lack of confidence, he passed the school exam in one go: a great feat! He greeted it with a shout of joy, praising Professor Domenico Bulferetti, who later confessed how moved he was by the young man's deep understanding of Dante. Thus Pier Giorgio prepared for the more difficult but already longed-for level of the Polytechnic.

Healthy, robust, he was the only one in the house to ride Parsifal, Father's fractious horse. He rode him for miles. I was longing to have a photographer ready to record my jumps and maneuvers. Pier Giorgio, instead, looked for children to give them a ride, or read the Gospel out loud, or stopped Parsifal to make the sign of the cross in front of a church.

We were beginning to be adults, but his character did not alter. He did not lose his genuineness. By this time he had joined the St. Vincent de Paul Society, an association dedicated to serving the poor. This was the beginning of his social work among people, done without anyone at home knowing anything about it.

Personal
Connection

CHAPTER 6

Social Struggle in 1919

Pier Giorgio was seventeen and emerging from adolescence, but it was difficult to begin adult life in 1918. Like so many young people, he felt the desire to shout, to get involved in politics, and to take part on one side or another.

It is not easy today to realize the deep divide that existed between the Catholic Party and the Liberal Party, from which Catholics kept their distance so as not to become contaminated. Liberalism represented "revolution", so it was not possible to support it: it had to be opposed "as the sin of the new century, as final impenitence, as direct, satanic, incorrigible opposition to the faith".

Catholics and liberals in Piedmont were on two sides of the barricades. And living in the house of one of the most fervent and important liberals of the time, even though he never joined the party, Pier Giorgio decided to adopt the Popular Party's position and promoted its paper, *Il Momento*. Although a little harsh and severe, our father's reaction was understandable and summed up in a short, meaningful warning: "That means when you're hungry you'll go and eat at *Il Momento*." But as a man of considerable personal prestige, Alfredo Frassati was not deeply disturbed, calling it a slight disagreement. On the other hand, for my brother, taking this position against the political ideas of our house meant setting himself against a society, a class, a mentality, crossing the Rubicon.

Our father's liberals, however, were those who had pleaded against Italy's hasty intervention—"renegade traitors to be shot in the back"—but the long, cruel war had, of course, proved them right. They began to raise their heads again and, with them, *La Stampa*, whose circulation had heretofore markedly decreased. Our father returned to bombarding from the front page of his paper the two chiefly responsible for this calamity: General Luigi Cadorna and Salandra, the prime minister.

Apart from these reprisals and criticisms of the imprudent and over-hasty entry into the war, rendered even more despicably useless by the sham peace, what was the general situation? The Socialists—some of whom were warmongers, future Fascists, and then Socialists again—proclaimed the revolution with grandiose articles, caricatures, and satires. They announced that the liberal bourgeois state was finished, and therefore they refused to participate in the government. Continual strikes, called for any reason, paralyzed national life. It only needed someone in the station to shout: "There's a priest on the train!" for the train not to leave the station. "There's someone with clean nails!" shouted another in another station, and immediately the drivers decided it was absolutely impossible to continue the journey with a bourgeois on the train. And then what happened? One bold spirit in a black shirt [a fascist] turned up and the train left.

In this climate, but in opposition to all extremism, the Popular Party was born. Its members agreed that their common task was to defend the rights of the workers, but it soon broke down into factions and internal strife. One shouted against Don Luigi Sturzo, its leader, another against the hoped-for electoral reform, which would also have given women the vote. Another protested and called all men and women to a Catholicism free from political activity. In spite of this, the party, which had been formed from the most heterogeneous elements, at least in appearance, continued to prosper. Meanwhile, the problem of the returning soldiers hit the country head on. It was difficult to take up studies again, get a job, or get clients back after four years of such a cruel vacation. It was difficult to shake off the spirit of violence that had developed. These were the heroes of the first pages of the *Domenica del Corriere*. Now they expected something more solid from life.

As an Italian opposed to the restoration of the Papal States, with Rome as capital, and, worse still, the Latium subject to a temporal power, useful only to distract the popes from their spiritual duties,[1] Pier Giorgio did not allow the often mediocre atmosphere of his university club, Cesare Balbo, to lead him astray. He felt the urgency of going out toward the disappointed masses, not only to build up support against political enemies, but in order to try to heal the situation. For the masses who went about waving the red flag, he thought that the necessary social reforms should be enacted, so that poverty would disappear and the standard of living return to normal.

At the university too, with its avalanche of irregular students, the climate was anything but serene. Pier Giorgio met hundreds of new companions, differing from one another in feeling, experience, and behavior.

The new environment is well pictured in this letter from his friend Curio Chiaraviglio:

November 21, 1919

Dear Giorgio,

. . . Give me news of your studies and when you will be going to the University and your first impressions of this

---

[1] The province of Latium was seized in 1870 by Italy, and the Papal States ceased to exist.—TRANS.

elite of the nation, that is, the university youth. I hope you will have better luck than I. Our first lesson was chemistry. I arrived pretending to be a serious person with a bag of books on my stomach, pushed into my trousers. They had told me it was not chic to go to the University with books in your hand like at school. I meant to go there with a walking stick of my father's, but luckily as I was leaving the house I happened to see myself in the mirror and my youthful looks made it obvious that the stick was not mine.

When I got to the University the first person I met on the stairs was a very good friend who, being a year ahead of me, thought it was his duty to give me a "pizza" on my head as a sign of welcome. This made my hat sink down onto my nose and the books slide into my trousers. I took it quietly either because I was embarrassed by the books or because of a certain respect I had for the sur-roundings.

I entered the semi-circular hall amid an infernal noise. The old students were honoring us by throwing clumps of grass and earth at us from the back benches. To save our honor in return, we smashed a seat to pieces and replied to the attack. I had the good luck to grab the straw seat and make it fly straight at the head of a young woman (unintentionally, of course) who fortunately managed to avoid it.

You can imagine how greatly my brilliant action was admired and at the height of honor they all concentrated on me. I will not tell you the "doings" of those five minutes. I was saved by the professor coming in, when everything calmed down. As soon as I had sat down I began to pull my tattered books out from my trousers, from the bottom because they had dropped to my feet. I was greatly admired by my neighbors, who found me very original.

This was my first and last chemistry lesson because the professor was so boring he made you fall asleep. It is also the last time I put my books in my trousers.

I have related to you my entry into the Athenaeum, because I think you too may imagine that there are so many serious persons there and find instead a bunch of hooligans. This of course is something that very often happens.

For his part, Pier Giorgio, with his background as a rich man's son, had to get on with the easy-going and penniless youths among whom he found himself. Silent, keeping to himself, he studied his surroundings and, little by little amid that welter of names (in one single course there were four hundred war veterans), he became known as the student who never refused to help. He was punctual but not a teacher's pet, calm, and uncommonly kind. Slowly, the derision he had met at first was transformed into respect. "Here's the senator, let us behave", said his companions, interrupting their frivolous and ambiguous talk. If they did not stop, Pier Giorgio used to break up the atmosphere of frivolity by starting to whistle. His whistle, like his laughter, was an alarm bell.

Pier Giorgio wasn't role-playing a modern-day Padre Zappata [a revolutionary Mexican hero], but lived a life of virtue. People who spent time with him naturally came to respect his personality as a consistent man, and not an abstract preacher. All in one go, he had overcome the dangers and temptations of his eighteenth year, engaged in works of charity and the apostolate, particularly among the young. In this he often relied on the friendship, experience, and collaboration of the monitor-custodians in his university.

* * *

A significant turning point in his life was his joining the university's Catholic club, called Cesare Balbo. [The club was named after the Piedmontese historian and statesman who died in 1853.] When the then-president [and future prime minister] Pilade De Nicola invited him to join, he was underage and could not do so without obtaining his family's permission. Naturally our mother, who had strong reservations about the members of Catholic Action, was not pleased. As "a good artist" she judged members of Catholic Action to be squalid and unattractive. We do not know whether her conversation with Pier Giorgio was heated or calm. But what we do know is that, after having hurried to Valsalice to confer with Don Cojazzi, she agreed to her son's wishes, even though unenthusiastically. So, next day, Pier Giorgio was able to return his membership form signed by his Catholic mother, for lack of his father's consent.

No one realized that the Cesare Balbo increased Pier Giorgio's detachment from the family. Now, away from home, his joy, purity, humility, simplicity, and faith led him to the apostolate. In the club, he was often surrounded by mediocre people. However, their very mediocrity made them ready to follow, and he ended up a leader. Those luminous eyes could look any man or woman in the face without his having to lower his eyes. He shook hands with new and old comrades, without reserve or visiting cards. No one realized, no one if asked then would have said, that he was everything to the club and totally committed to the club.

The people of the Popular Party, who later had to decide on his request to join their ranks, were afraid for a time that he might represent a fifth column. His request lay waiting while, in 1922, his religious and political creeds were investigated (in 1925 it was endorsed by the signature of Alcide De Gasperi). This suspicion seems absurd but, perhaps, justified by our father's fame as a liberal.

Pier Giorgio's decisive and brave behavior was in contrast

Pier Giorgio and Luciana in Berlin, 1922

Pier Giorgio (in light-colored jacket and black student's hat)
marches alongside the flag he and others defended from
the assault of the royal guards, 1922

to the reserve of others. He never removed the crossed shield (the emblem of the Popular Party)—worn in the buttonhole upside down by the Robottians[2]—not even on the extremely dangerous first of May of those years. When they came face to face with him, even the most violent adversaries were silent.

One evening in the Martinetto district, a group of women began shouting hostile remarks at a Catholic procession that concluded a welfare evening. Pier Giorgio went up to one of the shrillest and calmly asked her why she was so angry. He received in reply a rough-voiced account of the usual story of misery and humiliation. He did not say anything. He pulled from his pocket a piece of paper crowded with addresses and wrote the woman's on it too. She lowered her head and said no more.

He could not be persuaded to take off his Catholic Youth badge when he entered a Fiat factory notoriously dominated by revolutionary workers. His friend Chiaraviglio was frightened for him. But the workers did not lift a finger, did not raise their voices. They respected his presence in tense silence, which was their acknowledgment.

When he talked of soldiers, his face lit up. Not that he wanted to be even a corporal. Unlike bourgeois boys compelled to put on the gray-green uniform, he only wanted to be the equal of all, one of the boys.

Once he met a soldier from the Alpine Brigade during Sunday Mass, and, as they were going out, he approached him with a smile. It was Gianni Brunelli, with whom Pier Giorgio, competently and passionately, launched into mountain talk. As he was taking his leave, he invited Brunelli to gather a small flock of soldiers every Sunday and lead them

[2] Father Filippo Robotti inspired a Catholic movement.

to church. The following Sunday more than twenty men of the forty-first company received Communion.

He was always interested in soldiers, especially those who, when the war was over, were approaching demobilization. He attended their clubs to speak about getting back into civilian life after the tragic parenthesis of war. He was deeply aware of their problems. Indeed, if it had been resolved properly, the Italian political situation would have been completely different. War creates not only heroes but displaced persons. It was therefore necessary to help these soldiers regain their place in society so that they would not become disruptive elements.

At the time, withdrawal and indifference might have seemed a more comfortable option. Nevertheless, the moral duty was clear: to choose a trench, a barricade, a flag. And his first flag was peace.

One morning in 1919, Pier Giorgio went down into the piazza wearing his Goliard beret [a beret of medieval origins that students wore, with a different color representing each faculty] and shouted: "Viva Wilson!", a reference to the American president who raised such hopes for lasting peace with his dream of uniting all peoples in the League of Nations. Pier Giorgio shouted all day and went home hoarse. But he was well aware of the reality. He wrote:

> In the world there are so many evil people and even many calling themselves Christian, but in name only, not in spirit. I think peace will be a long time coming. But our faith teaches us that we must always keep on hoping we shall enjoy it one day. Modern society is wracked with the sorrows of human passions and is moving away from any ideal of love and peace.

In his opinion, the crisis was part of the much greater religious crisis. Pier Giorgio's work was never confined to mere political struggle and revolt. He was against violence, although determined to fight and die, if necessary, to defend Christ. His favorite saying, which he also repeated in letters, was: "When all accept Christ's voice and teaching, we will be able to say we are equal and every difference between human beings will be annulled." Any other way was short-lived and would easily fail. This was shown by the war, which was a consequence of the disappearance of the Christian spirit. So, for him, living in society meant struggling for the Spirit to return, reactivating it where it was feeble and kindling it where it did not exist. Politics was above all an act of faith, even though the times, the struggles, and the fighting made it sensational.

CHAPTER 7

Family Life

A large corner room furnished with great Piedmontese baroque pieces greeted us every day at mealtimes. Two windows opened onto the Corso Siccardi and one onto the ancient Piazza d'Armi, which was already being invaded by villas and mini villas blocking the view of the mighty Victor Emmanuel II monument.

A dark walnut chimney-piece filled the whole wall next to the door that led to the study. The flowerless terrace linking it to the dining room and the fireless hearth seemed like the emblem of our family.

Our father

When our father slammed the door, more punctually than the hour striking, I felt a sense of joy, for I could then interrupt my studies. He was intolerant of the slightest delay and immediately went into the kitchen. After having "saved" the pale cutlet from disgraceful contact with vegetables, he sat down at table without waiting for anyone. Indeed, impatience was one of his constant prerogatives. At any small irritation, he created a whirlwind of tragedy around himself, but, on the whole, he kept quiet and did not afford us a single glimpse into his life, which would have given us a window on the world.

When he was not silent, or making forecasts that the Ametis family kindly judged as never coming true, he indulged in his three V's: *vino* (wine), *vacche* (cattle), *vanga* (gardening). He imbibed his measure, discoursing subtly on its quality to the tepid interest of us, his companions at table, almost all of whom were teetotalers. The argument suddenly changed color and became white. "That cow produces four and a half gallons of milk!" General silence. Bovine life was a matter of indifference to us, remaining abstract because our father was incapable of making his audience share in his passion.

Another question was suddenly launched at the maid: "Is the salad from Pollone?" If the reply was in the negative, he suspended for a moment the loving gesture of drying it with his napkin and a veil of sadness glazed his eyes at the thought of the useless garden, which he visited regularly every Saturday.

Thus our father forced us to absorb as sole spiritual nourishment those problems which represented a tiny parenthesis in his life: livestock, the cowshed, dairy, and the mountains, which we scanned with a telescope, admiring the growth of the fir trees. Our father spoke of justice and equality between men and women, and, in the same breath, he said he expected his son to work and earn a living whereas I was to do nothing. Then he broached the sacred subject of his will in a solemn tone, which I tried in vain to make less tragic by a couple of caresses. He continued to speak of equal rights and death, but as one speaks of the living, with the attitude and the intentions of the living. And he usually ended by saying that, at home, questions of money did not arise, without realizing that he was the absolute arbiter, and all of us, including our mother, had to defer to his wishes without any right of reply.

Our mother

When we were all grown up, perhaps the saddest time during her day was when she was at table. In spite of her proverbial appetite, she sometimes seemed to swallow with difficulty, her throat constricted by crying. Taking advantage of our father's predilection for me, I sought some expedient to clear the heavy and electric atmosphere. It was not easy, however, to chase away those thick clouds at mealtimes. Only once, Pier Giorgio, dismayed by the tension between them, stopped the painful duel with a dry *"Basta!"* [Enough!], which fell like thunder. An icy coldness or scornful rejection greeted any proposal by our mother, such as the request to buy a beautiful piece of furniture or a splendid Favretto "at only three hundred lire". First, her congenital inability to keep accounts was attacked. She got her revenge on the rare occasions when Grandmother Frassati was invited. At those times, the only person who inspired us with a sense of complicity was Grandmother. We could not understand why our father tolerated his mother being treated in this way. Perhaps because he was weak in the face of discord and detested the effort required to bring things into the open.

Before the half hour for dinner was over, we heard the noise of a chair being scraped on the floor above, and Pier Giorgio announced that our aunt had finished dining upstairs, pleased that he could offer our mother the opportunity to go up and see her beloved sister.

For her exit, she made the usual excuse of a headache. Then, in the company she most enjoyed, that of her calmer sister Elena, our mother could tranquilly smoke her Tuscan cigar, which our aunt's subtle sense of smell found bearable. Aunt Elena was always ready to follow our mother in everything that pleased her, and our father valued his sister-in-law as an efficient administrator of the domestic finances.

Thrift was a way of life. Here is an example from a letter from our aunt to Mama. It was written when my mother was ambassadress to Berlin and our father's role was to "spend for the honor of Italy".

Turin, February 21, 1922

> I have had to send Pier Giorgio's gray overcoat to Celeghin. It is all worn out—pockets, cuffs—belt turned in green and the worst part of it is that he has not got the same material to repair it. But he will try to make adjustments by taking off the pockets, making cuffs and all for fifty lire . . .
>
> Let us hope that the fine weather will come: then he can go out in his jacket. But there is another problem. He cannot go on wearing patched clothes. He goes through them in no time. But his health is good and that is the main thing. I hand you over to Pier Giorgio's scrawls.

The parting dig was normal and so was the absence of all praise for my brother's modesty. He was always careful to avoid spending on himself and from boyhood had found everything too good for his person.

Luciana ← Author

My place was at our father's side. He suffered all vexations with Christian resignation: a spoonful of turnips thrown quickly onto the plate so that our mother would not notice, a pinch given at an appropriate moment, a brave request for funds that lit up Pier Giorgio's face, doubly satisfied if I was victorious.

In the secret duel between the house of Ametis and the house of Frassati, although I was thoroughly persuaded that everything depended on the will of the Ametis and that will was inexorable against the unfortunate person who opposed it, I sided with our name. I saw our father as the most immediate victim. What right had they to say and keep repeating that the Pollone house, the garden, and livestock belonged to the Ametis, that the gardener was their servant and so my father could not and should not give orders directly, that he, and all of us, should be careful not to send out the cards on which, erroneously, next to the name of the Villa Ametis, the name Frassati intruded?

I happily disobeyed this last order, proud that the beautiful house where I was born should bear my name and determined to combat the subtle contempt with which, for one reason or another, the certainly not common Frassati lineage was put down. I was always observant and ready to pick up a paternal expression of sadness or joy, behind which I divined *La Stampa*, the world I loved best and loved as one loves a flag. Perhaps because of this I regarded Pier Giorgio with some compassion because he dedicated himself to certain poor newspapers of no account. For me, *La Stampa* was the world of the finest, most intelligent and honest man on earth.

Did father feel all this? Perhaps not. He never went deeply into anything, but he liked me in his own way and he was proud that I had chosen the same faculty as he, Law. He was manifestly astonished with my results to the point of writing to me: "Congratulations! In total you have got higher marks than I." It was truly extraordinary for him to compare himself to a mere mortal. In fact, when he wanted to pay Pier Giorgio a great compliment, perhaps the only great compliment of his life, he wrote to him: "I see with pride that what little good there is in my character has not been lost."

Father's nearness at table gave me security, but being opposite Mama made me uncomfortable. Now though, the old fear of her weeping, which for years accompanied my every evening, has given way to an infinite sense of pity.

Pier Giorgio

The one considered least important in the family was the first to be lost forever. The two Frassatis stood facing each other but divided by an abyss. One was all transcendence and the other all pragmatism. But this would be a summary judgment of both and unjust to Papa. Count Carlo Sforza, the statesman and diplomat, said to me one day in 1948: "Your father always sees what there is, never what isn't." On the other hand, Pier Giorgio, living in God, always saw what was beyond, and everything he said and did proceeded from that vision.

What did they think of one another? Pier Giorgio was too faithful to the fourth commandment to allow himself to judge his father. He admired his tenacity at work, his loyalty to his political beliefs, the brilliant ascent and the decorum with which he managed to sustain difficult positions. One day he sent him this letter:

Turin, October 26, 1922

I heard recently that you have received the highest order of knighthood, after the Annunziata. I congratulate you and I am pleased that after such a long time you have been rewarded for your work that you do with such scrupulous care.

But my brother was different from him in every way. His detachment from *La Stampa* was evident. He saw the evil in the crime news and tried to point it out one day. "Sales also depend on those columns", was father's reply. And no more could be said.

It could not be said that wealth had changed the household's simple habits. Pier Giorgio was spiritually remote from all luxury and wealth. He had the great merit of having chosen the most difficult life when the easiest of lives was available to him. There was a sense of detached respect between son and father. "Pier Giorgio fills me with awe as if I were talking to someone older than myself. I don't know what it is, but, I repeat, he sometimes fills me with awe", he confessed one day to his editor Cassone. One evening both came home late. Our father reprimanded Pier Giorgio because he had not let anyone know and could have caused worry. My brother's succinct reply, "But where I was there was no telephone", was enough to satisfy completely someone who certainly was not returning from nighttime Adoration.

Our father had not realized that the quiet boy was upsetting all his plans with his own personality. He thought he could move him like a pawn with his strong will, which did not take others' feelings into account. Pier Giorgio was the male heir, and the house of Frassati would lose its full glory without him. But gossip began to circulate about his "pious virtues". And our father, although he did not give these rumors excessive weight, often showed irritation.

Berlin, February 1922

Dear Giorgio,
[By] always acting without reflection on things that should be extremely important to you (as in the special case of forgetting the book you needed for your next exam) you will become a man who is useless to others and yourself.

Your father

To avoid passing a final verdict on him we tried—and, exceptionally, Mama was with us in this—to keep Papa in the dark about little day-to-day incidents because, as he did not consider the reasons for them, he would not admit any extenuating circumstances and would immediately condemn Pier Giorgio.

                                           Berlin 1922

> You must persuade yourself, dear Giorgio, that life needs to be taken seriously. The way you behave will not do for yourself or your family, who care about you and are very distressed by all these things that happen too often and are painfully and monotonously repeated. I have little hope that you will change, although you really need to change immediately: take things in an orderly way, always think seriously about what you should do, have a little perseverance. Do not live by the day, as thoughtlessly as any blockhead. If you care a little about your family, you must change. I am very, very upset.

These words sound absurd today, and, if I had known about them, I would have condemned them with all my strength, even though I was only aware of a tiny part of my great brother's consistent and exhausting occupations.

Pier Giorgio had one single good point in the eyes of our parents. He was considered loyal and certainly not dangerous to the family fortune. This was in spite of the fears expressed when our parents had surprised us playing cards.

To praise what he considered the maximum expression of filial respect, our father once said about a friend of ours: "He is so good that he would marry whomever his father wanted." "Well, he's stupid then", was Pier Giorgio's prompt comment. His tone of dismissal struck our father dumb. These rare outbursts showed how he really feared Pier Giorgio, as is proved by a confession he made to one of his employees. "I have never accepted any order, not even from Giolitti. Only one person has had authority over me, and that is my son."

No one knew what a silent sorrow it was to Pier Giorgio that my father lacked religious spirit. No one ever heard him speak about it. He was reluctant to speak or ask him anything. The first time he openly asked him a favor, sure of being granted, was on July 3, 1925. His words and behavior appeared calm, in spite of the paralysis he felt. Pointing to a plea that came out of his jacket pocket, he said: "Here, Papa, to be published in *La Stampa*."

There was never any thought of rivalry between us. Our mother's obvious detachment from me, balanced by Papa's special tenderness, served to create a single front, in which we used our respective privileges for mutual defense.

Ever since he was a child, Pier Giorgio refused candies if I was deprived of them as a punishment, whereas the humiliations he suffered wounded me deeply. I was never flattered by prognostications like that written by Mama: "Even when he is forty Pier Giorgio won't have half the good sense of Luciana." A part of a letter serves to show our relationship:

Berlin 1921

Dearest brother . . . you know that your worldly sister enjoys going about . . . and company. The good God willed that I should have only defects and you many virtues. What is to be done? You will pray to him for me and I will too, with the little I am, but from my heart. And so we go on.

I liked success; he liked poverty. If anyone reminded him of his surname, he reacted with hurt and as if defending himself from an attempt to separate him from those he considered closest to himself. "But I am poor like all the poor", he declared to a bricklayer in Pollone, who was surprised to see him studying continually, considering his wealth.

I loved the glory of *La Stampa*. Pier Giorgio arrived at the paper soaked through, hardly better dressed than the poor who had to resort to the "Saturday charity", and he was obliged to borrow money to take the tram. Because of him they prophesied about the paper: "You of *La Stampa* will never do badly because you have a saint at home."

But no one tried to know him, not even our mother, at whom Pier Giorgio looked with great tenderness and, perhaps, despairing pity. It never occurred to her, for example, to inquire further into the real reason he came late to meals. He had run home to save the tram money and arrived so sweaty that he had had to change his shirt before he sat down to table. To his "Sorry if I am late, Mama", she replied with a reproach that basically meant: "You are fundamentally good for nothing, so you could at least arrive on time."

Pier Giorgio's silence finally confirmed her opinion about her son, whose mind was preoccupied with so many problems: a future to shatter and rebuild with religion, poetry, social duty; a fortune to find for the miseries of others. These were problems beyond her ken, not through lack of heart, but because they were not in line with her caustic mind, which considered any dilemma as the useless philosophizing of neurotic people. The things she said to her son, whom she also adored, were few and always the same, so that it was our mother who was the source of his mistaken reputation of being of modest intelligence, made worse by the accusations of his being untidy and distracted.

One of Pier Giorgio's sayings remained in the annals: there had been talk of sweet peas, and then the talk had moved on to politics, when Pier Giorgio came out with "we'll put them all in a window box", which sounded paradoxical but a "logical" conclusion to neutralist appreciations of Cadornian generals. The other accusations were unfounded stories, which did not, in fact, diminish his solicitude for our mother, with whom he had many tastes in common.

Pier Giorgio loved sometimes to take a sip of Marsala from her glass after meals, an unheard of thing since we had grown up without any alcohol at all. He had also learned to appreciate the strong smell of tobacco. Neither my father nor I was permitted to express annoyance at that cloud of smoke, and, if I complained, Mama retorted by calling me "delicate", a sure sign of her contempt. Proud of his smoking mother, a custom unusual among women, my brother tried a cigar in the garden at Pollone with his inseparable friend Camillo Banzatti. Banzatti felt ill after a few puffs, whereas Pier Giorgio stood the test brilliantly. Much later he became a placid smoker of Tuscan cigars (the cheapest and smelliest Italian cigars). If anyone asked him the reason for his bad taste, he replied, smiling: "Even my mother smokes Tuscans." Or he proudly explained the origin of his innocent vice by saying: "My mother smoked over me when I was being fed at the breast." His love for her never held recrimination.

When he came back from his night adoration of the Blessed Sacrament, he never forgot to reassure her by putting a little note under her door: "Dear Mother, I am home." But only after his death did she remember this:

> I can witness that he was always kind and patient in any family upheaval and according to his friends at school and in the University Circle. Both as a boy and a young man he mildly accepted any remarks of mine, the just and also the unjust ones. For example, I always told him he was wasting his time, without realizing all his activities in

doing good and forgetting even those I did know about. He not only accepted the reproach but never tried to excuse himself.

He never tried to defend himself from any of these accusations. Who would understand the greatness of his secret life? Humanity was his problem, which is why his mind often wandered as he went on eating calmly with an appetite that never let him down, as serene as if all the criticisms were addressed to someone else and as if there was perfect affection between those at table. No one minded when he silently refused some tidbit because it was Lent. They only teased him when he did not take any of the pudding that "trembled" or fish whose skin he could not tolerate. Until one day, in one of those final meetings, Mama suddenly said: "Pier Giorgio, do you know that Don Borla said they are talking from the pulpit about you?" "Nonsense, nonsense", was the reply.

CHAPTER 8

In Germany

Even the daily coming together at meals, which was some-times painful, came to an end. The close of 1920 brought novelty into our family life. Our father was appointed ambassador to Berlin, and we moved there for a while. Pier Giorgio faced this new world with an open mind and practical spirit, although he knew it might be difficult to carry out his mission there. "I hope I will get to know student circles and Catholic workers. Then I will be able to carry on my Turin habits", he wrote to Grandmother Frassati from Berlin on March 17, 1921. On the same day he told a friend that he had met Father Karl Sonnenschein. Of his long conversations with Pier Giorgio and their long walks on the outskirts of Berlin, only a few traces remain in my brother's letters.

Concise, cold at first appearance, Father Sonnenschein, who became known after his death in 1928 as the St. Francis of Berlin, gradually warmed up when people entered into the broad sphere of his social and religious interests. Nevertheless, our mother merely asked him for a written testimony after Pier Giorgio's death. This remained short and unfinished because of the thousands of tasks in which the priest was engaged. However, Pier Giorgio found Father Sonnenschein's German experience very important. He finally understood that in Italy, Sonnenschein would have had a difficult, or even impossible, time. They would have cried scandal when, for example, he was seen accompanying a girl picked up outside a nightclub to the house of his trusted friends. The conventional and prejudiced atmosphere of Italian towns and country would not have allowed a priest to live among the harsh realities of life, as Sonnenschein always did. My brother realized that, to carry out this German priest's noble mission in Italy, it was necessary for him to remain a layman. In civilian clothes, but a priest at heart, Pier Giorgio set out at the end of 1921 on the road of apostleship, which brought him ever closer to the interests of the dispossessed.

Meanwhile, with the sense of how transitory all things human are, the thought of death seemed to grow in him. He seemed already to have resolved it when someone advised him not to choose the mines as the sphere for his future work. He replied with a large smile: "Why not think that we will be much better off in the next world?" And saying goodbye to a fellow student, Anna Palomba, who was leaving Turin for Trento, he said to her: "We'll meet again in Paradise."

His stay in the Rahners' house was important for him. It seems incomprehensible that Pier Giorgio, who had the ambassador's residence at his disposal, should go off to Freiburg im Breisgau to deepen his knowledge of the Germans and their language. What attracted him was the very different atmosphere in the professor's house, recommended to him by Sonnenschein. He felt completely at ease there and became attached to the whole family, fully sharing their lives, even celebrating their birthdays. He offered to help the mistress of the house with her housework, including picking and carrying vegetables from a faraway garden. If ever the ambassador's son had been seen by officials in Berlin or by his family when he was carrying potatoes, they would have been surprised. And it is Frau Rahner who confirms that it was his experiences in Germany that made Pier Giorgio decide not to become a priest. "I want to be able to help my people in every way," he had told her, "and I can do this better as a layman than as a priest, because in our country priests do not have as much contact with the people as in Germany. As a mining engineer, by giving a good example, I can act in a more effective way."

But this did not lessen our mother's anxiety. She increasingly associated herself with our father in considering Pier Giorgio a failure. Now she felt he was missing out if he did not share in the social life of the embassy.

I was disappointed not to have him as a companion in my amusements, but found that Pier Giorgio not only had no share in my glittering life but increasingly sought to avoid it. I could not understand, because it was quite alien to me, his option for the poor and for militant Catholicism. I did not know about the frequent meetings, visits to the poor, and his charity directed at that time particularly toward the huge crowd of people who had fallen on hard times through the war and toward the people reduced to ruin by the collapse of the Mark.

Whatever my brother managed to save or take away from the embassy's sumptuous dining table, he distributed among his protégés. He went from one hovel to the next. He ran home, swallowed a cup of coffee, and rushed off to a hospital, to return finally in the evening, tired but content.

The "receptions" he attended did not require any formal attire, and they did not have music and dancing! One day, the chancellor of the embassy, Rofi, seeing him rushing out, asked if he was going to some party. He answered by giving the address of an alley near Alexanderplatz, a street full of misery. And he entered those grim houses begging their pardon, shy in case he was disturbing people, never forgetting that he was a stranger to them.

Encouraged by his gentleness, they all asked him for help and favors. If it was a question of letters, he always answered, he responded positively to everyone's requests and noted in the margins "replied". Unheard-of precision in our house!

His presence in Berlin, though irregular, did him good because it gave him a break from the studies he still had to do in Italy. Returning one day, after a journey in a third-class compartment, he sat down smiling at table, at which Peppino Garibaldi and an extremely beautiful American lady were guests. Though Pier Giorgio was smiling, our father was not. It was not clear to me what was going on. Only twenty years later did I hear that he had arrived in Berlin, where the temperature was twelve degrees below zero, in a jacket because he had given his overcoat to someone who did not have one. Our father, although a generous giver, found the gesture exaggerated, and it confirmed once again that he had a somewhat odd son.

What help was it to Senator Frassati, ambassador of the king of Italy and proprietor of *La Stampa*, to have a son who carried away the flowers from drawing rooms to put them on the coffins of the poor?

Displeasure at my brother's absence from a brilliant social life explains how proud I was to be able to write to Grandmother Frassati one day: "Tomorrow evening we are all— including Pier Giorgio, who seems very pleased to be in Berlin, it is a pity that he is staying such a short time—going to *Rigoletto* sung by Battistini."

My brother often grumbled about what he considered a waste of time, but he did not give up his interest in the arts. He loved Verdi, even though for our family the god of music was Wagner. His interest surpassed that of us all when one day in Prague he rushed to hear Smetana's *Two Widows* and, passing through Vienna, *Don Giovanni*.

Although, like all of us at home, he sang out of tune, in church, in order to satisfy the great desire he felt to express himself in song, he tucked himself away in some hidden corner so that he would feel more at ease. If it was necessary during a procession, he opened his mouth and would sing for the whole square, not minding the people who told him, "You are out of tune." He replied: "But the important thing is to sing."

He loved art and during his travels he visited museums and galleries, collecting in several fat albums reproductions of the works he most admired. However, he did not let art get in the way of his student duties, religious practices, or option for the poor. His work for the Pax Romana[1] led the Austrian representative, Miss Schwan, to write: "You carry the Pax Romana not only in your mouth but also in your heart."

Profoundly convinced of the necessity for unity among Catholics of all nations, and influenced by the experience of Sonnenschein, who was one of the major organizers of Catholic students and workers (in Germany there was not one single large official association as in Italy, and this priest's group was the biggest), in July 1921 Pier Giorgio took part in the tenth national congress of FUCI [Italian Catholic University Federation], held in Ravenna, together with the Dante celebrations and the first meeting of the Pax Romana.

---

[1] An association founded in Fribourg, Switzerland, that had as its purpose the unification of all the Catholic students throughout the world to cooperate in the construction of peace.

CHAPTER 9

Action in Rome

The peace that Pier Giorgio had always hoped for now assumed a religious force that thrilled him. He greeted people with "*Pax tecum*", and in letters we hear words like these: "When I think of the Pax Romana, I am always afraid that it will remain only on paper. I hope that God will again open the hardened hearts of the men who sow hatred." And again: "If all peoples were to have inner spirit, Pax Romana would bring peace and justice."

As a result of his experience in Germany, at Ravenna Pier Giorgio proposed the fusion of GC [Gioventù Cattolica; Catholic Youth] with the FUCI. The FUCI was the product of so many struggles within the universities, struggles undertaken and sustained by a series of admirable sacrifices.

In the years of anticlericalism and positivism, when the Freemasons intervened, sometimes in disgraceful and provoking ways, in the assignment of university chairs, the Catholic students had formed their own clubs. Those who dominated this university association [FUCI] did not want it to become a section of the Catholic Youth, an organization largely made up of workers, peasants, and employees.

Pier Giorgio's idea was revolutionary enough to scandalize the bourgeoisie, who were determined to remain well separated from others. Born of a bourgeois family, with a bourgeois education and links with bourgeois society, he insisted, with the tranquil security inspired by his faith, on a permanent union between students and Catholic workers. He hoped that the people picked would thus become leaders of a real and serious elevation of the working classes. He was against the FUCI, not in itself, but because it bore fatally the marks of classism and was in danger of becoming the instrument of the upper classes, with restricted interests and ulterior motives.

His daring proposal was totally blocked by the speech of the chaplain, Monsignor Pini, in favor of FUCI's isolation, contrary to a more modern social activity. So the few Fucini belonging to the Catholic university club Cesare Balbo were defeated.

The tall, blond, and curly-haired Monsignor Giandomenico Pini had been a lawyer, and he had the gift of captivating the young. Many addressed him familiarly as "*tu*" and they sang to him: "We say yes to Monsignor Pini, you are the mother of us Fucini!" He lived for the young and sacrificed himself, but he did not realize the need to anticipate the changing times.

Pier Giorgio's social work, on the other hand, appeared progressive compared to the ideas put forth at the FUCI congress at Ravenna. When he joined the Popular Party he sided with the advanced wing. Someone who travels third class and takes the cheap seats in the theater so as to offer the difference in ticket price to the poor cannot side with the forces attached to money. Someone who has espoused the option for the poor cannot belong to the conservatives. Pier Giorgio's balanced outlook made him always hate factions. He branded his opponents with irony rather than hatred. "To that one," he said, alluding to a conservative M.P., "let's send some naphthalene, so he'll be better conserved."

Central to his social thought was agrarian reform: distributing the land to the peasants seemed to him the greatest conquest of the religious spirit over the world's selfishness. Anyone who teased him by asking: "And what about your lands?" he answered promptly: "They are nothing to do with me; they belong to my father."

When Carolina Masoero, an elderly and wise servant, warned him against agrarian reform because it would reduce him to poverty too, he replied: "And what does it matter?"

But these things seemed like dreams. And, like all dreams, they came up against the reality of facts. Even Fr. Sonnenschein's efforts to prepare the young for mixed social life had no success. The calamity of Hitler was about to break upon Germany and the world.

* * *

After the FUCI congress at Ravenna, Pier Giorgio and other participants went to Rome for the celebrations of the fiftieth anniversary of the Italian Catholic Youth. After the papal blessing, the young people formed a procession to pay homage to the Unknown Soldier. They had only gone a few hundred yards when a group of provocateurs started shouting: "Long live the Pope King!" A general confusion arose and fighting broke out.

Naturally, the royal guards appeared wielding muskets to disperse the assembly. Pier Giorgio threw himself into the throng to free a feeble friend from their hands.

By God's will the clash calmed down and the procession continued until it reached the Chiesa Nuova. Here the police had set up the first barrier. A mass of fifty thousand young people, however, cannot be stopped that easily. The first obstacle was easily overcome, and the procession led by the Emilian and the Piedmontese Fucini continued toward the Altare della Patria [unknown soldier].

But a second barrier awaited them: a cordon of royal

guards ranged in the Piazza San Pantaleo and Piazza Argentina. This time it was much harder to get through, and there were some incidents. All at once, in the Piazza del Gesù, the cavalry of the royal guard turned on the procession and charged. Kicks and blows flew. Some youths fell and were hurt, but others managed to proceed through the Via del Plebiscito.

The goal seemed at hand when more guards poured out of the Palazzo Altieri under the command of "the most sectarian police officer I have ever known", as a friend of Pier Giorgio recalled. The order given to the royal guards was, in fact, imprudent to the point of madness: "Take the flags." The guards attacked, beating people with rifle butts, breaking the poles and ripping the banners that a few hundred young people were stubbornly defending. The struggle seemed unequal.

The first flag to fall into the hands of the guards was the flag of the contingent from Trent (yellow and blue with a black eagle), which was violently snatched from the hands of its bearer; then, one by one, the other flags fell until the guards laid hands upon the Cesare Balbo tricolor. The breathless standard-bearer remained with the broken pole in his hand. Then Pier Giorgio seized the trampled banner, while the charge of the royal guards flung him beyond the church steps.

Thus my brother's whole group, who still clenched the glorious piece of cloth, found themselves in the Palazzo Altieri courtyard, which was functioning as a giant security chamber. There, finally, the young men could embrace one another. Every now and then more friends arrived, driven from the brutal fray in the Piazza del Gesù, and were welcomed in Pier Giorgio's brotherly arms: "Zanone, you too ended up here? Keep calm, though, keep calm!"

And he encouraged and reassured his excited companions, above whom he waved the banner of their greatest hopes, the flag in rags. Many had clothes torn and quite a few were wounded. A priest was knocked over in the courtyard, his cassock torn. With howls of protest the young people mobbed the police, but fresh guards were suddenly upon them. A Sardinian who did not want to surrender the flag was threatened with a bayonet. Pier Giorgio intervened. He almost threw himself at the lieutenant who had permitted such a disgrace, shouting at the top of his voice our father's name. As if by magic, the officer changed his behavior, severely rebuked the soldier who had threatened the Sardinian youth, and politely asked Pier Giorgio to go away. But he flatly refused to leave the courtyard alone and preferred his flag to the freedom offered him because he was an ambassador's son . . . or, rather, the son of the powerful owner of *La Stampa*. He sat down with his friends, chatting with them, and comforted Dino Donelli, who was crying. Then he knelt down in the courtyard beside the injured priest, and, holding up the rosary, he invited all to prayer, "for us and for those who have hit us". In his other hand he still clutched the banner of his club.

He was considered the hero of the day, a glory that he himself rejected: "As soon as I read Renato Vuillermin's [1] editorial I felt very angry because he had falsified things in that way, speaking openly of two or three of us when all had behaved in the same way."

So the exhortation to modesty sent him by Gian Maria Bertini [a friend from his club who later became a priest] appears totally superfluous:

[1] Renato Vuillermin, regional president of the GCI [Italian Catholic Youth], was shot by the SS in the Sant'Angelo fort at Savona on December 27, 1943. He died shouting: "Long live free Italy!"

Turin, September 15, 1921

I must speak to you as a brother about Vuillermin's report and warn you once and for all to be careful because people tend to be a bit partial with you, and it is not hard to guess why. I was indignant especially because Vuillermin had tried to make your action stand out. That's fine! But he did not have a single word for Sanpietro. That poor lad deserved praise, as perhaps you too deserved it. And yet there is absolutely nothing about him. This is called taking advantage of the situation.

I thank you for the blessing you implored for me: what venerable behavior you adopted on September 14!

I'd be very pleased if you remembered a postcard or two for my sister.

Regards from Isidoro Bonini.

Bye. Be contented and charitable.

Gian Maria Bertini

P.S. From time to time think that while you enjoy yourself millions of others are suffering, so do as much good as you can.

To these unprecedented warnings were added "invitations to make reparation", with the added concern for the group who borrowed glory from him, praising him only after his death. "The Boninis wanted your address. Perhaps they will write to you. Be sympathetic. It is worth it." Would my brother be annoyed if I added that it would not have been a matter of friendship but of practical advantage for them?

They wrote to him shamelessly, warning him to become better. But this was not something to make Pier Giorgio lose his smile and his energy. Father Filippo Robotti, O.P., knew him well. He went off with him to promote Christian ideas in the Communist outskirts of Turin. Good nerves and firm fists were needed, because hecklers usually passed from words to "action". To those who complimented him on his courage, he replied: "It was necessary to remain and not show any fear. We stayed, that's all." He also sometimes took the risk of going out at night to put up political posters in public places.

His friends begged him to be careful of Fascist factions. There was nothing to be done. Knowing how cowardice opens the way to violence and injustice, he replied: "One ought to go and one goes. It is not those who suffer violence who should fear but those who practice it." Or: "When God is with us we need not be afraid."

CHAPTER 10

The March on Rome

Blessed are those who hunger and thirst for righteousness

The year 1922 is fixed in every Italian mind because of an event that had fatal consequences: the march on Rome on October 28 and the coming of Fascism to power. Most of the young who believed in the gospel opposed the power of the "black shirts" [the Fascists] with courage but insufficient means.

Taking part in a procession at that time meant risking insults or even blows. But still the streets of Turin saw Pier Giorgio go back and forth, along the lines winding after the holy images. A militant Catholic, he regarded it as an obligation to be present at all religious demonstrations. He sang and prayed out loud in between two rows of closed, hostile faces. In the procession for the Eucharistic Congress there was a dispute between two Fucini, which he calmed down at once with a sonorous: "Praised be Jesus Christ." Farther on, some young men with the Fascist badge in their buttonholes began sneering offensively at the Fucini's homage to Monsignor Balestrina, patriarch of Jerusalem. Pier Giorgio immediately burst out at these provokers to ask what they meant. His friends had to stop him while the Fascists went off.

He also became familiar with prisons, where, in witness to his faith, he was often "remanded" following encounters between police, the royal guards, and the Fucini. He was

Cardinal Gamba in procession in Turin, 1924

detained for a few hours, during which he intoned the rosary. Then, when they discovered his name, they made haste to bring him before the head of the police. Then the real battle began. Pier Giorgio protested energetically against the police force's inhuman methods. He only used the name Frassati in order to be able to give his own reasons and those of all his comrades in the faith.

When it was not processions with their obligatory ending in detention, there were congresses. At one of these, held at Piscina, Pier Giorgio arrived by bicycle at eight in the morning. People noted that the ambassador's son's clothes were dusty from the tiring bike ride. When asked why he had not come by car, he merely shrugged his shoulders with a smile.

At the congress of Piedmontese Catholic Youth, held at Novara, Monsignor Gamba met Pier Giorgio and was struck by this young man who had fasted until late in the day and was asking him for Communion. When appointed arch-bishop, he came to Turin two years later and instantly recognized Pier Giorgio among the others.

At this congress there were no clashes because the Novara authorities had organized a Fascist meeting on the same day on the Lago d'Orta. Pier Giorgio arrived in the city with a flag and some pamphlets, for whose printing he had had to sign a bill of exchange. He hoped to sell a few copies of his *Cantiamo Fucini* [Let Us Sing Fucini]. What would our father have said, who boasted that he had never touched that dangerous piece of paper in his life? But there was no danger of Father finding out because, when it was a matter of charity, Pier Giorgio became a cunning diplomat and never talked of it to anyone who might betray him. So no friend of the family ever discovered his "crime", that is, no one who was incapable of understanding it.

The special train driven by Catholic drivers who had offered their services for the congress on their day off was the occasion of a generous gesture by Pier Giorgio. He went from carriage to carriage, beret in hand, collecting money as a practical sign of gratitude. This time, too, he had disguised the generous gesture as a humorous bet: "Will you bet that the train manages to go sixty miles per hour now?" Then he ran back along the train, happy and lighthearted, without boasting, inviting his companions to recite the rosary. When the Fascists waiting for them at Santhià started yelling, he raised his powerful voice and shouted: "Long live the Catholic railway workers! Viva!"

These were the weapons that Pier Giorgio gave his friends to affirm their moral strength. Even though the cudgels of the police might have done a better job, the young Catholics' seriousness and diligence always prevailed. But they were idealistic assertions of spiritual power. The cudgels continued to beat, the politicians went on ranting in vain, and in the end, the two chief victims were liberty and Italy.

Pier Giorgio's sorrow was great. All his letters from this period refer to the situation with great sadness.

> Let us hope that our country can have an administration capable of making itself respected that finally puts an end to the great scandal that is the Fascist movement.
>
> Nevertheless even here the dear . . . Fascists have arrived, called naturally by the country's great patriots, the administrators of the Banca di Sconto. They forced the mayor to resign; thus Pollone's debt would increase, having to pay an employee to look after the affairs of the town until the next elections.

And just when Giovanni Giolitti was wondering: "What good can come to the country from a marriage of Don Sturzo-Treves-Turati",[1] Pier Giorgio wrote:

> I place my hope in a Popular-Socialist ministry. I can understand the violence to which unfortunately the Communists still resorted in some countries. But at least they were for a great ideal, to raise the working class, who had been exploited for so long by people with no scruples. But what ideals do the Fascists have? Filthy lucre, paid by the industrialists and, shamefully, also by our government. They act induced only by money and dishonesty.

Mussolini came to power on October 28, 1922, the day of the march on Rome. It is easy to imagine Pier Giorgio's sufferings. Our family was spending its final period in Berlin because, with the ascent of the Fascists to power, our father resigned from his ambassadorship.

[1] This was a reference to Don Luigi Sturzo, the leader of the Popular Party, Treves, and Filippo Turati, the leader of the Socialist party.

That day Pier Giorgio was invited to dine with friends. After the meal, which became charged with an atmosphere of resentment because of Pier Giorgio's criticism of the weakness and vacillation of the government that had finally allowed the Fascists to take over, the group set out for Santhià. Instead of acting as a tranquilizer, the train was a stimulus. No sooner had Pier Giorgio sat down in the compartment than he began loudly to discuss the situation, saying that Christianity, a religion of love, absolutely could not agree with Fascism, a doctrine that exalted force and violence. "He was raving", recalled his traveling companions. And a comic moment occurred when a group of Fascists got onto the train to ask for money for their organizations. They rushed out of the compartment occupied by Pier Giorgio, stopping for a moment at the door to threaten: "You don't give now, but later you will."

Pier Giorgio never changed his attitude from the day of the march on Rome.

A little later, he rejoined the family in Berlin. But he was still in great distress:

Berlin, November 19, 1922

I glanced at Mussolini's speech and my blood boiled. I am disappointed by the really shameful behavior of the Popular Party. Where is the fine program, where is the faith which motivates our people? But when it is a matter of turning out for worldly honors, people trample on their own conscience.

I'd like school not to start again. I'd like to have my degree so that I could stay in this beautiful country where people still feel a sense of responsibility and have a conscience.

Today, more reluctantly than ever, we should recognize

that the Christian poet Dante was right and still is when he exclaims:

> O house of grief! O bond-slave Italy!
> Ship without pilot in a raging gale!
> No mistress-province, but a stews and sty!

And later:

> Write something about the Popular Party, because I heard many voices in Rome and I'd like to learn the truth, to know how to behave this year.

Until the coup d'état in 1925, it did not seem as if Fascism had definitely won power and installed a dictatorship; it seemed like a transitional phase, probably of short duration, which would serve to "put things back in place". In other words, people had convinced themselves, or at least "right thinking people" were convinced, that Fascism was a cheap and useful broom to sweep the Communists out of Italy. Naturally, once they had been driven out, again according to these smug people, the broom would be thrown in a corner. Even Count Carlo Sforza maintained, against Frassati, that the fall of Fascism was a question of hours or, at the most, months. Our father won the bet he made in 1923, as is attested by a fine Chinese vase that still graces the house in Pollone, proving how utterly wrong the Count's pious wish was.

Gossip circulating about the Popular Party, saying that it might fuse with the Fascists, infuriated my brother. He wrote to Tonino Severi, his friend from FUCI and Cesare Balbo:

> I don't like your ideas about the Popular Party a bit! I think: better alone with a clear conscience than together with all the others but a large stain on the conscience.

His just hopes were disappointed. On October 31, 1922, the Partito Popolare Italiano leadership issued the following declaration:

> The leadership, having received information of the attitude of the leaders of the parliamentary group in the solution to the crisis of the ministry, reveals that beyond the course of events, today the conscience of the Country is bound to seek a return to order and internal peace, respect for constitutional liberties, economic reconstruction, the true base of economic prosperity, the reorganization of the work forces in the collective life of the nation, but harmonized and connected to the supreme interests of the country, and finally and above all the revitalizing of the moral values of civil life in fellowship, which can have no other foundation for us than Christian.
>
> In the gruesome climate of these hard days falls the fourth anniversary of our victory. May the memory of it serve to spur the wills on to another victory, that of the economic and political reconstruction of our Italy with respect and in freedom.

Almost at the same time, the press published the names of the two ministers and the four under-secretaries of the Popular Party who had become part of the Fascist government. Pier Giorgio's great sorrow that year was seeing people he respected in cahoots with the "band of rogues".

Going against the
Popular opinions

My Model Is Savonarola

Blessed are the meek

Pier Giorgio turned twenty-one in 1922, but his coming of age was certainly not accompanied by the usual fanfare. On this occasion, our aunt Elena wrote to our mother:

Turin, April 6, 1922

It is Pier Giorgio's birthday. The poor boy has had a very lean day of it. Yesterday I went out to get him some flowers, a few anemones, some lovely freesias, some chocolate creams and pastries, to give him a bit of a celebration. I felt sad that he was spending his twenty-first birthday alone with his worn-out old aunt. Then in the evening he had a friend over and they sat looking at minerals that he had picked up in the mountains until half past eleven. This morning at eight he was sleeping like a baby, and I woke him up with a kiss from you all.

Today I have hardly seen him—school—then to Signor Farina to draw—meeting—lesson with the teacher who is helping him—he rushes in late with, "Excuse me if I am late, Aunt." He is well, and now he no longer has the tram season ticket; he goes by bicycle, and I think this gives him a better appetite. He will have to study a lot and needs to keep his strength up. I try to look after him as well as I can. He is always happy with everything.

From Berlin Pier Giorgio continued to receive sermons from Mama: "Please remember that your studies and your health are more important than all your clubs." "Do not forget that little bit of Italian. I hope you will have used the time to study and prepare your drawings. Do not waste a minute. Think that you may have to do the exam and try to be as well prepared as possible."

And the same from Paris after Pier Giorgio had put off an exam: "You know how much it upsets me that you are always putting off exams. You never do anything on time." And she concluded by writing to her sister: "You know that talking to Pier Giorgio is a bit like talking to the wind."

The exams, the daily tasks that he punctually and wonderfully fulfilled, that is, his visits to the poor, were "nothing". And again: "You are always deceiving yourself and losing track of time. Leave off your visits and everything (that is, the club, conferences, and nighttime Adoration) and do what is your duty. Very sad altogether."

And Aunt replied:

> You did well to lecture Pier Giorgio. I have already done so, but he always has an excuse: if he did not go to Turin he could not prepare himself in so many things that he thought he had understood. If he had gone on the first call he would have failed. And the end is always that when he says a day it means a fortnight later. Now there is nothing but to hope we shall see the end of these exams and meanwhile hope that he will . . . mature.

Such perplexity was expressed together with the news of success at playing solitaire! Again our mother writes: "That studying when you are dazed with sleep is useless and bad for your health. You would be a good boy but you are so stubborn."

The tune never changed. They accused him of wasting time, being stubborn, even of lying, without taking into account the wealth he was accumulating, whose value eluded our father's administrative rigor and our mother's aspirations. He was accumulating treasures for the day on which the final account is rendered.

Marianna Cerutti, a poor woman who polished the floors at *La Stampa*, said to our father: "Your son will have a better career than you!" Marianna, a Socialist revolutionary and friend of the poor, knew many things about Pier Giorgio's secret life. She knew whose homes he went to, when he jokingly told her he went out to make his "conquests". She knew the network of good works that trapped him in the city. Study was only part of his day and, although he considered it his first duty, he often came to it only after a considerable time spent with the poor, a session at the St. Vincent Conference, and a night spent in Adoration.

This did not make him study any less hard, or fall into the temptation of pulling a few strings in order to pass the exam. When a friend, Guardia Riva, asked why he wanted to take such a difficult degree as engineering, seeing he wanted to be a missionary, he replied that without a professional preparation he could not keep his apostolate effective. Study was very hard work for him, but he did not give up.

His modesty never allowed him to boast about himself. He preferred to admit publicly to "my poor mental abilities". He would say, "So and so is much more intelligent than I." "But I am not a bit intelligent." "I am a Biellese" [meaning: stubborn].

It was not a pose. His humility was constant and absolute and never left him. Anyone he was with, rich or poor, was his neighbor. He possessed the humility of the wise, which comes from knowledge, and, even more, from knowledge of the Lord. In an arrogant world his position was the most logical and closer to God.

* * *

This humility led him to two spiritual affirmations: an act of faith and an act of charity.

The act of faith was made on May 28, 1922, in San Domenico church, which was festively lit for the centenary of its patron. There he took the scapular of the Third Dominican Order, assuming the name of Fra Gerolamo, which was the first name of the Dominican martyr Savonarola. To anyone who greeted him with that name he replied: "May I imitate him in the struggle and in virtue."

He shared his enthusiasm with his friend Antonio Villani, who wanted to follow his example:

> I am so happy that you want to become part of the big family of St. Dominic, "where is", as Dante says, "good fattening if there be no wandering".
>
> This name recalls a figure who is dear to me and certainly to you too, as you share my feelings against corrupt morals: the figure of Fra Gerolamo Savonarola, whose name I most unworthily bear. I am a fervent admirer of this friar, who died as a saint at the stake. In becoming a tertiary I wanted to take him as a model, but I am far from being like him.

Even the choice of name shows a state of mind, a conscious preference for the work of purification and renewal. It explains better than anything else the scope of his vocation, interwoven, to use the words of Father Ceslao Pera (an eminent Dominican in Turin) with élan, combat, and conquest.

* * *

Pier Giorgio was forgetful of the family's economic position. He did not consider his father's fortune his own and said he did not have a penny. He was not lying either to himself or to others. His wealth was never more than the few lire that our mother gave him from time to time, and it was quickly distributed around Turin, as it had been in Berlin. "I see a special light surrounding the poor and unfortunate, a light that we do not have", he explained to a companion.

He was never bored or tired. Leaving by Corso Galileo Ferraris, Pier Giorgio went off to his secret life in the Via Santa Chiara, among the sick of the Cottolengo, among the old in the home for the aged. The frequent note in his notebook: "6 o'clock, by the Consolata clock" refers to the departure point for so many of his peregrinations.

But in order to help he also needed money, quite a lot of money. And who gave it to him? Our father nothing, our mother little. Often he borrowed a bit from one or the other, and he was the only one in the house obliged to keep accounts.

One of the many pages in his notebook is the moving proof:

November 26, 1923

—For the Women's Club L10, that I owe Cesare Balbo
—Paid Giovanni Gola his journey to Novara
—For the mountain hut Rocciamelone L5, that I owe De Nicola
—Boarding house meal L1, that I owe De Nicola
—Ices for Spataro L6, that I owe De Nicola
—Tertiary badge L3, one of which I owe Fra Alberto Caligaris
—L5 to St. Dominic, that I owe Don Borla
—L24 for the Club

Considering our education and our manner of living, Pier Giorgio, acting as he did, showed a rare courage: he went against a principle considered as sacred, the danger of debt, which in our father's moral reckoning smacked, if not of dishonesty, at least of the height of irresponsibility. And then, what about family dignity? How was it possible, being a son of Frassati, to beg loans from everyone? In fact, few were the people from whom Pier Giorgio did not beg small loans, even from those of lesser means. But the poor saw a light in him.

Pier Giorgio's very courtesy was a charity. Those in the know—from school teachers to people he had just met to domestic servants—all experienced his unselfish kindness, which was expressed toward his fellow students by giving them his books, saying that he had too many, paying university taxes, arranging tuitions. He is well remembered at the Polytechnic, especially by the porters, who were in his confidence and often surprised him intent on his good works at the Cesare Balbo club and with Fucini friends.

In the summer, everyone went to the sea or the mountains. Pier Giorgio went back to Turin as soon as he could, happy to be with our father and to tramp the streets under a scorching sun while the asphalt melted under his shoes, in order to continue his charitable works.

He belonged to many conferences of the St. Vincent de Paul Society, and he often found himself in delicate and difficult situations: split families; illegitimate children; men with criminal records. He was not scandalized. He remembered Christ's warning: "Let him who is without sin cast the first stone." He hoped for the end of certain forms of charity conditional on the "good behavior" of the recipients.

> Carlo [he writes to his friend Bellingeri], if you want to know what I think, I would abolish certain Conferences of St. Vincent. When they have people living in the past and full of Christian zeal, who do not even know how to warn the parents of the supposed conduct of their daughters and try to do good works, but instead prefer to

abandon the family, it is better the Conference should not exist. Not because these people act in bad faith, but because this is not appropriate for today.

He had a great love for the sick, from whom one day he would contract the fatal polio. It was among the sick that he had found the best opportunity to share his humanity, and it was among the sick that he reached the end of his human pilgrimage.

CHAPTER 12

I Believe

Blessed are the peacemakers

In the years when Pier Giorgio was developing and extending his plans for social work, the threats of Marxism and Positivist Liberalism became daily more and more persistent.

> The times we are going through [he said to the young] are difficult because cruel persecution of the Church is raging. But you bold and good young people should not be afraid of this small thing; remember that the Church is a divine institution and cannot come to an end. She will last till the end of the world. Not even the gates of hell can prevail against her.

Pier Giorgio managed to speak of these grave problems almost as one speaks about ordinary things. He had that gift of simplicity which enabled him, even in spiritual matters, to pass naturally from the serious to a joke, from a smile to communion and prayer.

His deep faith explained certain of his attitudes, which were otherwise incomprehensible, such as his apparent indifference to his father's liberal atheism, his renouncing of a love of his own, and his acceptance of continual humiliations.

> Our life, in order to be Christian, has to be a continual renunciation, a continual sacrifice. However, this is not difficult, if one thinks what are these few years passed in

suffering compared with eternal happiness, where joy will have no measure or end, and we shall have unimaginable peace.

We should grasp faith strongly. Without it what would our whole life be? Nothing. It would have been spent in vain.

These are unusual words for a young man, but his deep awareness had advanced him in age. Living in faith expanded his short life and enabled him to lead a life of charity, exercising his apostolate as well as living the normal life of a man and a student.

The faith given to me in baptism suggests to me surely: of yourself you will do nothing, but if you have God as the center of all your action, then you will reach the goal.

Once he had understood and mastered this truth, Pier Giorgio felt really at peace. He could do nothing, if not in the Lord, and from this certainty he gained the strength to continue a life so different from his education and family background. He got from Communion the energy to face the day. His passions were mastered and every difficulty, every obstacle to right living, was overcome. He said in a speech to the Catholic Youth of Pollone:

Feed on this Bread of Angels and from it you will gain the strength to fight your inner battle, the battle against passion and all adversities, because Jesus Christ has promised to those who feed on the Holy Eucharist eternal life and the graces necessary to obtain it. And when you are totally consumed by this eucharistic fire, then you will be able more consciously to thank God who has called you to become part of that multitude, and you will enjoy the peace that those who are happy in accordance with this world have never experienced, because true happiness does not consist in the pleasures of the world or in earthly things, but in peace of conscience, which we only have if we are pure in heart and mind.

He went to Communion nearly every morning. He escaped to church, usually to the Crocetta, and, if he could, he served Mass. After Communion, people tiptoed past him because he was often gazing upward, sometimes in tears, kneeling on the ground. Characteristics of his faith were certainty and absolute trust in prayer. In many of his letters he asked for prayers for himself or promised his to others:

> I ask you to pray a lot for me, because I desperately need from God the grace to carry out my projects to good effect. . . . Only prayers can obtain from God the desired improvement.

And again:

> Luckily a great Justice exists beyond; if a good and just God did not exist, our life would be useless.
> Will I have the strength to get there? Certainly faith is the only anchor of salvation. We should cling to it tightly. What would our life be without it? Nothing, or rather it would be spent uselessly, because in the world there is only sorrow, and sorrow without faith is unbearable. But sorrow lit by the torch becomes a beautiful thing because it tempers the soul to the struggle.

They sound like words of farewell. But his faith, with its message of life, remained.

* * *

Pier Giorgio was hit hard by the 1923 crisis in the Ruhr region. As he wrote to his friend Villani: "The occupation of that bit of Germany is a disgrace because it ruins the most Catholic part of the German population", and moreover "within two years, I too, if God gives me life, will go to work in the Ruhr. As a Catholic, I will help the Germans as much as possible." At that time he had to limit himself to expressing his disdain for the occupation and his solidarity with friends in Germany, sending to the Catholic Youth of Bonn the message published on January 13, 1923, in the *Deutsche Reichs Zeitung*, entitled "The Conscience of the World Awakes":

> In these tragic and painful moments when your country is trampled by foreign feet, while your adversary is occupying your hearths as an enemy of your country, we Catholic students send you this expression of our fraternal love. We have no possibility of changing the sad situation, but we feel in ourselves the whole force of our Christian love, which makes us brothers beyond national boundaries.
>
> Governments today take no notice of the Pontiff's warning: True peace is more a fruit of Christian neighborly love than of justice. They prepare for future wars for all humanity.
>
> Modern society is sinking into the sorrow of human passions and is withdrawing from any ideal of love and peace. Catholics, you and we must bear the breath of goodness, which can only arise from faith in Christ.
>
> Brothers, in these new trials and terrible sufferings, know that the great Christian family is praying for you. Act so that your sufferings and struggles may be made easier.
>
> Since peace cannot return to the world without God, you at least, men of good faith, keep him in your hearts who was announced by angels in the cave to be the savior of humanity.
>
> Pier Giorgio Frassati
Circolo Universitario Cattolico Cesare Balbo

And to his German friend Willibald Leitgebel:

February 11, 1923

We, too, have lost the most beautiful and best thing that God has given to humans—that is, freedom, without which life becomes difficult. I would have liked to have done a lot for the Germans, but unfortunately I can do nothing. Please take this money for the poor children in Berlin: it's not a lot, but it's better than nothing.

The thought of death in these his last two years of life was continual and real:

Did you see the tragic end of poor Loretz [he wrote to Severi on the thirteenth of August 1923]? Unfortunately he was killed at the Château des Dames, a very easy glacier, which I scaled two years ago with the son of Carrel, the guide, without seeing any danger from falling stones. But this year because of the great heat the thaw is stronger and so the rocks are more easily dislodged.

This is what will happen to me in a few years' time. And the conclusion is: When one goes into the mountains one should sort out one's conscience, because one never knows if one will come home. But with all this I am not afraid, and thus I am keener than ever to climb mountains, reach the most difficult peaks, feel that pure joy that is only to be had in the mountains.

That summer, our uncle Pietro Frassati retired to Cossila to die there on August 23. He was a just man who never wanted anything for himself. Pier Giorgio was present during his final hours.

Our uncle, who loves me so much, was so moved when he saw me that today I am not going back to his bedside for fear of causing him too much excitement. But now my duty is done. Although unworthy I was the instrument, together with my good mother and sister, who are lovingly caring for him, of Divine Providence. I was able to make him do all the religious observances. I believe that when he received the sacred Host, tears of joy mixed with sorrow poured down my face. No sooner had he received the Host than God mysteriously calmed his suffering, and after that Uncle sent for the parish priest from his home, to show him the satisfaction of having received the holy sacraments.

God in his infinite mercy did not regard my innumerable sins, but heard my prayers and those of my family. He gave our uncle the great grace of letting him receive the last sacraments fully conscious.

Believe that this life must be a continual preparation for the next, because we never know the day and the hour of our passing.

Quote

Thirty days later, in memory of his brother, our father gave away to charity the million lire our uncle had bequeathed to us.

Neither Pier Giorgio nor I was allowed to dispose of it. "My poor would have been satisfied with a few thousand lire", was Pier Giorgio's only comment. He was twenty-two, without a grant, and without ever having a penny in his pocket.

Lacking both understanding and financial support from the family, along "God's way strewn with many thorns but also many roses" he met someone who had seen him only once but who nonetheless wrote to me while he was still alive:

Turin, August 13, 1923

You tell me, in spite of myself, the infinite torments me. Then you think of your brother, such a noble soul, all of whose energies are directed toward a higher good and you say: perhaps he alone in the family is in possession of the secret that leads to happiness. Nevertheless because of that perhaps he can cause distress in those who love him.

The wonder of a brief encounter with a similar great spirit demonstrated how much spiritual poverty Pier Giorgio often had to endure.

Pier Giorgio with friends at Rocco Sella

CHAPTER 13

Friendship

Blessed are the pure in heart

The time for long conversations was over and so the time for delays. Everything in these last two years of his life had to be put to maximum profit, because everything seemed like a last chance to Pier Giorgio. This included even the Sinister Ones Society, which he had dreamed up and created as a good work, without the members themselves being aware of it. "Sinister ones" and "disreputable" were two epithets in current Fucini slang. The motto of the society was: "Few, yet good, like macaroni". Almost automatically, the mountains were the preferred place for the out-of-town activities of the new society's members, who, chivalrously, appointed as their president Clementina Luotto, Professor of Letters, "the Irma Grammatica [a theater actress] of the well-turned phrase", as my brother described her.

One evening when they had been to a play by Gioacchino Forzano, *Il Conte di Brechard*, Pier Giorgio saw a remarkable resemblance between the role of Perrault and his friend Marco Beltramo. So the next day he greeted him with a resounding, "You are the new Perrault", which made his friend retort: "Then you are Robespierre!"

When the two nicknames were adopted, the "Terror", which was the principal and only subsection of the Sinister Ones Society, was born. They specialized in cracking jokes against their "co-citizens". This new "Terror" was nick-named the "Fracassi Company" by the Jesuit Pietro Righini. Their "exploits" often ended with a sack put in someone's bed, a little donkey sent to an unstudious member, scolding letters and hoaxes, but all of them carried out with pure Christian feelings that helped to create brotherhood. The members, however, followed no rules and attended no set meetings. Everything was improvised. The important thing was to be together as much as possible under the great ensign of the faith.

Pier Giorgio realized that the group's steadfastness could also nourish a common enthusiasm for the Christian apostolate. For this he used his favorite instrument, high spirits, which, in its various forms, flourished in the society, creating a collective spirit and uniting all under the magic sign of laughter. Only thus was it possible for such diverse personalities to remain close, for not all of them were aware of the regenerative values of the spirit.

One of the society's very few rules was to inform an absent member of the Sinister Ones' activities. So, when they were separated, letters, called "proclamations", began to pass among them.

The cheerful mountain trips were occasions for friendship. Not a single episode was missed in written accounts of these occasions. Pier Giorgio was a brilliant chronicler who had the gift of transforming ordinary facts and situations into transcendental events. Yet he was the one who had always been accused of not wanting or knowing how to write.

* * *

Within the loose structure of the group, with its events and customs, there was a higher goal, which rapidly vanished when Pier Giorgio died. It was his charity and lively spirit that had enlivened the group.

The fact that the small society contained young women and men did not diminish Pier Giorgio's prudence and extreme delicacy in confronting what in those days was seen as a problem—the mixing of men and women in the same social clubs.

On this subject, Pier Giorgio was clear and rigorous. He protested to the presidents and to Monsignor Pini himself when the relations between the two FUCI clubs—the Cesare Balbo club, which consisted of men, and the Gaetana Agnesi, of women—seemed to allow excessive intimacy. Postwar freedom had led to more socializing between the sexes, and the problem of "mixed company" was debated vigorously.

There was plenty of exaggeration, verging on the ridiculous, as this fragment of a letter from a Catholic youth leader shows: "If a painful necessity forces us girls to frequent the same schools as boys, let us at least try to avoid this disgrace in our meetings." The problem of this "painful necessity" was not evident or even felt by Monsignor Pini, who was accustomed to holding joint meetings, trips, and spiritual exercises, some of which he himself joined.

Pier Giorgio, who was accustomed to a life in common with me and my girl friends, to attending mixed schools, diplomatic circles, and political circles abroad, and to meeting with the families of his poor people, found female company completely normal. But he understood perfectly well that not all of the members of the group had the same education and mentality as he did, and he realized that mixed groups could sometimes lead to a lack of commitment.[1]

[1] So he sometimes protested: "I am angry with Grosso because the Cesare Balbo has too many contacts with the Gaetana Agnesi. He thinks that Via Principe Amedeo 26 is the headquarters of a mixed circle. Bit by bit the president will no longer be Grosso, but the Circolo's young women."

Some were afraid that the future general assistant of FUCI might end up distracting members too much from their studies, even though it is clear that the priest only intended to unite all the sheep under his fatherly care. Perhaps because of this disagreement, in addition to the debates that took place at the Ravenna Congress over uniting the FUCI with the Catholic Youth, there was no great understanding between Monsignor Pini and Pier Giorgio.

My brother's personality, spirited, but serious about important matters, is shown in this fragment of a letter written by Pier Giorgio and Tina Ajmone-Catt to Lea Raiteri, dated June 16, 1924:

> Dear Signorina . . . At the moment we are studying in Turin but our spirits are shaken by the monstrous things that are happening in Italy. We live in a state of agitation because we don't know what's coming next. Only our faith enables us to keep going.

And Tina writes:

> "Frassatino" who is here with me asks whether the problems with your family have been resolved. I have replied that you will turn it into an illness; he is laughing like a jolly fellow. Do you know what he is saying? "Say to Signorina Lea that she need give an account of her actions to God alone and that one day the bad will get tired of their back-biting. There is no need to pay attention to gossip, much less get ill by giving in to those who perhaps have never known what truth is. 'Act so that those who see your good works glorify the Father.' Thus Jesus says in the Gospel."
>
> Citizen Robespierre charges me to beg your pardon if he has not yet written, but he is so lazy and he also has to work out some tricks with Beltramo, which he finds more amusing.

* * *

One of Pier Giorgio's Fucini friends was Laura Hidalgo, secretary of the Society. She was the only girl for whom Pier Giorgio felt a special affection, growing out of the common works of charity. He met Laura at Little St. Bernard during the 1923 carnival holidays. She had been a D'Azeglio pupil when we were younger but, being older, had been there three years ahead of us.

Everything up there at Little St. Bernard made Pier Giorgio happy: the snow, which was always excellent, the simple life of the hostel, the mystical recollection in the chapel.

In this atmosphere he fell in love for the first time with the girl who, though an orphan, faced life with courage and success and also looked after and supported her younger brother. When Pier Giorgio returned to Turin, restrained by his reserve, he spoke to me of a lively, spirited girl, an intimate friend of Laura Hidalgo, whom he had met in the hostel. He begged me to ask them both to tea.

The visit, which, I realized later, meant so much to him, was considered by mother and me to be just an offer of tea and nothing more. It never crossed our minds to consider Laura, a student of mathematics, as the beloved of Pier Giorgio's heart. It did not occur to us even though the girl felt she was being cross-examined by our mother. But it would not have entered Mama's head to connect her son with any girl who, as she caustically expressed it, was a "Catholic Action girl".

We did not realize therefore that Pier Giorgio was watching Mother's reactions as intently as one awaiting mercy or condemnation, and it was up to me, more than a year later, to inflict on Pier Giorgio the negative verdict. With what trepidation he awaited it, as he himself says in a letter written in August from Forte dei Marmi, after he had been to Quercianella to meet Laura Hidalgo: "When I find the right moment to speak to my sister I will also tell the particulars of this visit, but for now diplomacy and my mother's poor state of health require me to be cautious."

Pier Giorgio spoke to me about this on December 18, 1924. The conversation is described in a letter of mine to my fiancé, with a painful picture of my brother:

> Yesterday evening he came to me with his great black eyes and told me he was in love with a girl I know. . . . Of course I have said nothing to Mama because it would be the final blow. Poor boy. It was moving to hear him speak. I told him to try not to see her. He told me he had already tried and added: "If I go to the mountain on Sunday she will be there too. How can I not go? Should I telephone her? Write to her?" Poor boy! I looked at him and realized it needed all his goodness, all his uprightness to act that way. And to tell the truth, I felt much, much worse than he did. He ended by telling his plans for the future and his ideals, tearing my heart by adding to everything he said: "I cannot, for I do not want to leave Mama."
>
> We must not forget this and treat him with great kindness and tenderness, as if he had said: "Luciana, I am sick." Giorgio told me also that not only had he not yet said a word to her, but that he had not even made the slightest allusion.

Pier Giorgio did not think for a moment of pursuing his affection for Miss Hidalgo against what he was sure was our mother's will, and he told me decisively: "I am the one who is sacrificed." At that time I could not understand the tragic reality of that sacrifice, underlined by what he had said on one occasion "even if it costs me the sacrifice of my earthly life".

The intensity of his love and his will to sublimate the painful renunciation emerge very clearly, despite his usual reserve, in this letter written to Isidoro Bonini:

Modane (Turin), December 28, 1924

I am reading the novel by Italo Mario Angeloni *Ho amato così*, in which he writes in the first part about his love for an Andalusian woman, and, believe me, I feel a lot because it is like the story of my love.

I too have loved like that, only in the novel it is the Andalusian girl who makes the sacrifice, whereas in my case I am the sacrificed, because that is what God wills. Today I am going to Sauze Oulx to try the Giovane Montagna track. Tomorrow the group is heading for "St. Bernard", and my heart and soul go with them for two reasons: first of all because "St. Bernard" is the cradle of my, albeit vanished, dreams and, secondly, because she whom I loved with a pure love and whom today I have renounced will be there too. Yes, I want her to be happy. I beg you to pray that God will give me Christian strength to bear it all serenely. And that he will give her every earthly happiness and the strength finally to reach the end for which we were created.

Pier Giorgio suffered hard and long for his lost love, as is revealed in a letter of March 6, 1925. He is replying to a friend's letter that sounds as if it had asked him questions with rude curiosity. My brother hints at the great strength of his repressed feelings:

Truly I have not talked to you about such a bitter subject. But this was not for lack of confidence but only because the matter is now over and it is better not to speak about it anymore, but to close this episode in my life forever. Yes, the tone of this letter will amaze you, but you must realize that something has changed in me. It is not my doing, because I did not carry out any of the firm measures I told you about before you left Turin. I have often been in the mountains with her, often with others. But then I decided that as I could not attain my objective, it would be better now to kill the seed which, if well looked after, could produce immense benefits, otherwise only grief. In my inner struggles I have often asked myself why I should be sad. Should I suffer and bear this sacrifice with a heavy heart? Have I lost my faith? No, thank God, my faith is still steady enough and so we confirm that which is the only Joy that can satisfy us in this world. Every sacrifice is worthwhile only for this.

Then as Catholics we have a Love which is above all others and which—after that we owe to God—is most beautiful, as our religion is beautiful. Love whose advocate was that Apostle who preached it daily in all his letters to the various churches. Charity, without which, says St. Paul, every other virtue is worthless. This indeed can become the guide and direction of our whole life, a whole program. This, with the grace of God, can be the goal toward which my soul strives.

Imagine if now, when my soul is going through this crisis, I had the misfortune of not believing. Life would not be worth a moment longer, and death alone would be the healer of all human suffering . . .

So, my program in this is to transform that special feeling that I had for her, and which is not wanted, to the end to which we must strive, the light of charity in the restful bonds of Christian friendship, respect for her virtues, imitation of her outstanding gifts, as with other girls. Perhaps you will tell me that it is mad to hope this. But I believe, if you pray a little for me, that in a short time I can achieve that state in prayer.

This is my program, which I hope with God's grace to follow. Even if it costs me the sacrifice of my earthly life, it does not matter.

These letters are also a witness to his total purity: a purity that marked his whole life, all his gestures, all his words.

One of his confessors, Don Carlo del Rey, the parish priest at Forte dei Marmi, said: "I am not betraying any secrets if I tell you that, in the month of August 1924, Pier Giorgio still wore the baptismal stole of innocence." His smile, ready to turn into loud laughter, testifies to this immaculateness.

Naturally, his gift of joy was not understood by all, though his smile remained proverbial.

* * *

During 1924, students taking the mineralogy course made a trip to Piacenza. Pier Giorgio's insistence that the time of departure should allow for the fulfillment of Sunday duties met with a dry refusal from the professor, Augusto Stella: "Here we are among students, not Marian Sodalists!"

My brother took no notice of the rudeness. He did not leave with the others, but rejoined them in Milan, after having attended Mass.

When they arrived at Piacenza and had visited the wells, while his companions thought about occupying their free time in not strictly cultural pastimes, Pier Giorgio coaxed Giovanni Griffa to go with him to see the new bridge over the Po. His friend was close to him because they shared a common passion for minerals, a passion of Pier Giorgio's since childhood. Even then he had come home with his pockets full, and would cram his sandals with stones, pebbles and crystals, using them as bags.

Carolina Masoero, the cook who honored her beloved "little master" after his death with thirty or so pages of precise information, full of feeling, wrote that my brother, at the age of fourteen, had told her about his harvest of minerals and insects "for which he had great interest and love, and sometimes he had pieces of coal which he called minerals and said: 'If when I die I have a valuable collection, I will leave it to the Museum.'" His desire was granted, and Professor Antonio Cavinato accepted the bequest for the Polytechnic, whose museum in Valentino Castle was later destroyed.

* * *

By 1924 the country was heading toward complete dictatorship. Not even the sometimes inconsistent Popular Party seemed prepared to oppose it. Pier Giorgio expressed his perplexity at the time in a letter from Freiburg im Breisgau on October 23, 1921:

> I am very sad that the PPI [Popular Party] only makes promises and so people are abandoning it. Let us hope that in the next congress it decides something firm, because Italy expects a great deal from this party.
>
> I read the program and I found a big mistake in the omission of agriculture, through which Italy will be reconstructed.

The letters his friend Curio Chiaraviglio wrote to my brother had taken on a tone of "high" politics, as befitted the grandson of Giovanni Giolitti:

> July 16, 1923
>
> Dear Giorgio,
> Yesterday I attended the funeral of the PPI parliamentary group. . . . As I know this interests you, I will give you a brief report. I know my point of view differs from yours, but I also know you tolerate people expressing their views, however strongly.
> At the beginning of the session (which lasted eight—interesting—hours), it seemed that the various factions were rigidly opposed to the vote for reform. I have always thought that the government would find fifty mean characters among the Socialists and the Populars

who would desert the chamber at the right moment, thus allowing the government to obtain a relative majority. But I was wrong, because they found more than double that number among the Popular Party. And thus the government won easily. Once again it has shown that great political events cannot be reduced to simple intrigue. When the opposition loses courage it is of more use to those who meet it than to those who make it. Thus yesterday the government won, whereas if the opposition had not behaved as they did, it would not have had this victory. However, I have the impression that the PP is in liquidation. Don Sturzo has resigned and is doing spiritual exercises at Monte Cassino and the group is dissolving. With the new law we will have 350 Fascists and all the other parties will divide 175 seats among them.

His fears were confirmed during the visit of the head of government to Turin, when the Cesare Balbo Circle gave in to expediency. On October 14, 1923, Pier Giorgio wrote to President Costantino Guardia Riva:

I am really indignant because the flag which I, unworthy though I am, have carried so often in religious processions was hung by you from the balcony to pay homage to one who gets rid of the *Opere Pie*, who does nothing to check the Fascists, and allows ministers of God, like Don Minzoni, to be killed and permits other disgusting crimes to be committed and tries to cover these up by putting a crucifix in schools, etc.

I took full responsibility and removed the flag, although late. As of now I send you my irrevocable resignation. I shall continue with God's help, even outside the Club, although I do not like this, and I will do what I can for the Christian cause and the peace of Christ.

I desire that this letter of mine written in haste but

dictated from the depths of my soul be read aloud at the next meeting.

And again:

To the governing council of the Cesare Balbo:

I am returning to you my card and badge, which no longer belong to me legally. I shall join the Catholic Action as a member of the Catholic Youth Movement, which conducted itself rightly on this occasion, and could not honor someone like the Head of Government, who is incapable of controlling his subordinates and allows them to break into clubs and harass the members.

One should not be surprised, Jesus Christ said: "The children of darkness are more cunning than the children of light." But he also said: "Beware of false prophets and wolves that come to you in sheep's clothing."

I beg you to judge this act of mine calmly. I have to do it to obey my conscience.

With deep esteem in Jesus Christ.

Pier Giorgio Frassati

The president of the Club, on the occasion of All Souls' Day, asked him to go back on his decision.

From Donato, 11/2/1923

I remember you with renewed affections, and I particularly pray to our dead to intercede with the Divine Providence so that the true Christian may return serene after the deplored tempest, unsought and unwanted by everyone. Yours in Jesus Christ,

Guardia Riva

Two weeks later, Pier Giorgio withdrew his resignation:

Dear Guardia Riva,

Severi has told me that my position in the Club is still
uncertain. So I will now clarify it. Because I do not want
to be misunderstood or my action to be interpreted as
opposition to a person or as having other ends, while still
vigorously protesting the hanging out of the flag, for the
good of the Club, I withdraw my resignation.

Even if we do not see eye to eye on some things,
believe in my affection in Jesus Christ.

Pier Giorgio Frassati

* * *

In June 1924 a tragic event occurred. In its attempt to con-
solidate its own power, Fascism had not hesitated to suppress
one of its principal enemies, Signor Giacomo Matteotti, the
Socialist deputy. At the news of his murder, Pier Giorgio
trembled with horror and hoped for a moment that the
shock that his innocent blood had been shed might help save
Italy. He wrote from Turin on June 21:

Dear Tonino,
At this moment, when evil has shown its most nauseating
aspects, I am thinking about the days we spent together. I
remember the first elections after the war, and the coming
of Fascism. Now I recall with joy that we were never for
Fascism for a single moment of our lives. We always
fought against this scourge of Italy. Now that this party is
heading for its ruin, we can thank God that he has
deigned to make use of poor Matteotti to unmask to the
whole world the infamous, disgusting, and hidden crimes
of Fascism.

He had prayed and hoped that the murderers would be
found, but the news brought with trepidation to the Club
was always negative.

I was in London, alone for the first time, but in the care of Marcello Prati, *La Stampa*'s correspondent. From Pier Giorgio, the only person who was worried about me, I used to receive letters urging me to "be very good" and saying, "I pray God to bless you and make you better and better", as if with these words he was trying to warn me, protect me. At the station, he had given me a rosary made with seeds he had gathered himself, which I still have today.

It was in London that a letter reached me from our mother confirming what I had read in the English papers about a strange Fascist attack on our house, thwarted by the courage of Pier Giorgio:

Monday, June 23, 1924

My Lucianetta,
Listen to what happened recently. I am telling you about it because you will read about it in *La Stampa*. Yesterday, Sunday, Papa left at 11 for Pollone. I said to Paola, come to Mass and lunch with us. We will be cozy and have a chat. The cook was late in serving lunch, not till quarter to one. We had not put a forkful of risotto into our mouths when we heard Mariscia, who had gone to open the door, screaming and crying. Pier Giorgio and I sprang to our feet. At the door he shoved me behind him. He went out first, then I did, and we saw a ruffian in the corridor who was trying to rip out the telephone. Pier Giorgio jumped at him and gave him a couple of punches, so he turned and escaped into the hall. Others also ran off. Pier Giorgio fought the first man in the hall, punching him from the door. He tore his truncheon (a dangerous weapon) from his hands, shouting all the while, "Hooligans! Cowards! Murderers!" I was screaming, "Leave him, Giorgio!"

One of the brigand's hands was free, and I was afraid he had a revolver.

As those scoundrels found Pier Giorgio so energetic, in a twinkling of an eye they ran away frightened. Mariscia had escaped from Pier Giorgio's study, through the drawing room into the dining room and shouted into the street, "Help! Help!" Paola was on the balcony. Pier Giorgio, seeing she had gone, shouted to me: "They have taken Mariscia!" and went downstairs to look for her. I shouted, "Giorgio, Mariscia is here." Italo, the chauffeur, was in the cellar. He arrived to find them on the stairs and managed to see the car that hurriedly took them toward the Corso Sommeiller.

They had broken a vase under the central mirror in the hall, taken down and broken those frames, and the billiard mirror. Nothing else. I think they hoped the flat would be empty so they could ransack it.

I have got over the fright now that it came to nothing and am pleased to have saved the pictures, tapestries, silver, etc. But I did have a couple of moments of fright: the worst was when we did not know what was happening and heard shouts and bangs like shooting: "They are murdering Mariscia!"

We rushed out, and I had the feeling "We are going to get shot by a revolver." The second moment was when Pier Giorgio was fighting, and I was afraid he would be hurt. So I shouted: "Leave him!" Really they were all "chicken". Or their orders were to be spiteful and break things but not to touch people.

You will see the story in *La Stampa* on Monday or Tuesday. . . . Italo, who has become a very important "Sherlock Holmes", as he calls it, went to the police to confer with the already identified "malefactors" (thanks to him the car was recognized). All in all a lot of fuss about nothing.

From all sides, congratulations poured in. "Only Giolitti", Mother wrote to me in another letter of July 1, "spoke to

Papa and did not even mention it. You can understand how my heart is thrilled when I hear so much praise of Pier Giorgio. Now whenever excommunicated and bad people dare to tease Papa that Pier Giorgio is a bigot, he will be able to answer that bigots know how to do their duty when the moment comes."

Count Carlo Sforza, the statesman and diplomat, enthusiastically telegraphed to Papa: "Congratulations from us both on a risk averted and congratulations to Giorgio, who has shown how, if you want, you can always be master in your own house!"

Pier Giorgio was certainly not pleased with his fame. He was profoundly pained to hear that one of the hooligans was the brother of a friend of his in the Club. He forgave him, saying that for the deed, or rather misdeed, he simply felt pity.

The immediate consequences of the aggression were spectacular: the chief of police was dismissed by Luigi Federzoni, who was the minister of interior of Mussolini's government in 1913, and for eight months some policemen watched the house, and another was given the task of protecting Papa wherever he went. His joy can be imagined. He did all he could to give the policeman the slip while Pier Giorgio took cigarettes and hot soup to the police on guard duty. When he was begged not to be seen going about so much at night, he answered: "I just take care not to have much money on me. At most fifteen or twenty lire, and if someone comes up to me I give him everything I have so they go away happy. I am not afraid, as you see, I come home at all hours."

Many could not understand him or appreciate his need to be joyful. They banished him, together with Marco Beltramo, for his lively reaction to a wordy conference for the Catholic Action youth:

The leaders [Marco relates] sat on the stage to give us their speeches in turn, while the members crowded the orchestra pit.

We, Fucini, were quite noisy, as usual. When the president of the Catholic Ladies had finished her long, monotonous speech, I climbed onto the shoulders of Pier Giorgio and Rivera (Ursus) and gave the Fucini "shout": "For the Turin Catholic Ladies a cannon shot; and another and a third and last." Each time, the mass of Fucini replied with a resounding "Boom!" Then finally I called: "And the Fucini echo replied . . ." and they let out a shout that was a mixture of whistles, shrieks, and howls. This was the tradition.

The success was enormous. While a large part of the assembly roared with laughter (in joining in the applause, PG forgot his supporting function, making me crash to the ground), the speaker looked pale and shaken. Severi, president of the Cesare Balbo, jumped up and dove into the pit with his face set for great occasions. He had a go at me and ordered me to leave the room, threatening me with other sanctions. PG intervened in my defense and insisted that he was partly responsible. Severi sent him packing too.

Next day at the headquarters of the Cesare Balbo, the president's decision was communicated to PG and me: expulsion for both, because of our excessive lack of discipline "and other jokes", which shed a bad light on the seriousness of the FUCI. PG and I received the communication with the greatest hilarity.

To the solemn letter of reprimand from President Severi, the two reprobates replied, joking about the stinginess of the man from Modena who had sent a single sheet addressed to Pier Giorgio, asking him to pass it on to Beltramo as well.

Pier Giorgio welcomed this rebuke with cheerful nonchalance. The laughter and the joking that might seem irreverent were, in fact, a breath of fresh air. At all costs he wanted to help the university students remain enthusiastic.

* * *

Joy also reigned at Christmas. It was the last one of his life. Pier Giorgio seemed wild with mirth. In the night, he and some of his friends accompanied Canon Bues into the seminary for the traditional *panettone*. During the function, his behavior had been angelic. His mystic rapture had detached him from what was happening around him. His companions observed with amazement that he had an even more rapt expression than usual. But, immediately afterward, he rushed down the seminary corridor with a friend to the canon's bedroom. The canon remained on the ground floor, trying in vain to control the noise of the other young people.

They plotted the refined torture of a short-sheeted bed, but, unfortunately for the bold conspirators, the door to the canon's bedroom was locked. They were forced to give up the attempt and merely left as a sign of their presence a "Happy Christmas, Canon—PGF and NRR [Nanni Ravera]" on the wall.

The following year, the canon invited his Fucini friends for Christmas again. For a long while the same joy reigned, even though Pier Giorgio was no longer alive. Someone thought of playing the same joke that Pier Giorgio had failed to carry out the year before.

They went upstairs cautiously and advanced along the corridor, but had to stop in front of their ecclesiastical assistant's door. This time, they were not locked out. The small inscription and the sign on the wall of their absent friend, about whom nobody had thought earlier that evening, froze them in their tracks.

But that evening they did not feel a real absence, because Pier Giorgio's spirit was with them. He had served midnight

Mass with them and then gone out afterward with them into the deserted streets of Turin among the illuminated shop windows where the joy of Christmas was reflected in other faces.

Pier Giorgio descending Mon Viso, 1923

Pier Giorgio atop a mountain, with three companions

Mountain climbing on Rocco Sella, March 19, 1924

Pier Giorgio on his last climb, June 7, 1925.
The note "Verso l'alto" on the photograph is his.

CHAPTER 14

Leave-taking—January 1925

Blessed are those who mourn

"Peace be in your soul": this is Robespierre's wish for Perrault for the Holy Year. Every other gift we possess in this life is vanity, as all the things of the world are vanity.

It is beautiful to live because our real life lies beyond, otherwise who could bear the burden of this life if there were no eternal joy as its prize for sufferings; how could we explain the admirable resignation of so many poor creatures who are struggling with life and often die in the breach if it were not for the certainty of God's justice?

In the world that has gone astray from God there is no peace; it also lacks charity that is true and perfect love. Were we to heed St. Paul a little more, human miseries would diminish.[1]

It would have been a year like any other if the Vicar of Christ had not opened the doors of Justice. No one at home thought of anything extraordinary; no one spoke of that door which would be opened in Rome for the Holy Year of 1925. To Pier Giorgio, that year had also brought the bitter renunciation of his love. It was a painful time for him. This fragment of his letter to a friend attests it:

---

[1] Letter from Pier Giorgio to Marco Beltrano, dated January 15, 1925.

Unfortunately, one by one earthly friendships produce sorrows in our heart because those whom we love become distant, but I should like us to swear a pact that knows no earthly boundaries or time limits: union in prayer.

And how is your life going? Mine, as you can guess from the beginning of this letter, is perhaps going through the most acute period of a severe crisis, and just at this moment my sister is going far away, and so it will be my duty to be cheerful at home and suppress the gray mood caused by all the opposition I encounter. I shall be cheerful on the outside to show my companions not sharing our ideas that you can be a Catholic and still be young and happy, but internally when I am alone I give way to my sadness.

I had no doubts about advising Pier Giorgio to renounce his love, and I did not consult anyone about it. I did not reveal his secret to our parents, knowing how implacable they would have been against any aspirations that did not correspond to their desires. Pier Giorgio had moved me with his confidences about his love for Laura Hidalgo, but the days leading up to my marriage slipped away in concerns about my trousseau and emotions about my presents, which Pier Giorgio had barely glanced at: jewels, silver, pictures, but no Christian symbol. So wasn't marriage a sacrament? I, too, thought of it as a duty for life, but I did not feel it necessary to think too much about God and the saints.

After days of careful searching through the antiquarian shops of Turin, my brother went to the archbishop's house with a packet in his hands. Monsignor Gamba, the archbishop, was busy at that moment, and, while Pier Giorgio was waiting with Canon Rabbia and the servant Francesco, he wanted them to guess first what was in the packet: "A wedding present for my sister", and in those words he concentrated all his tender pride.

Neither of them could guess. At every suggestion Pier Giorgio smiled and shook his head. Finally, he unwrapped the crumpled newspaper and took out a splendid ivory crucifix. The canon and the future Don Francesco were stunned, but they saw such satisfaction in Pier Giorgio's eyes that they did not dare express what they were thinking: "A crucifix for a wedding?"

As soon as he was free, Archbishop Gamba came to meet Pier Giorgio, and the same hand that would bless the marriage was laid on the present. Later at lunch he spoke about Pier Giorgio, as he often did, with particular emotion.

At home, in contrast to the satisfaction that shone from Pier Giorgio's face at his successful search, I faithfully represented the family's feelings, although I did not show it. I was astounded by the gift, which was more suitable to the sadness of a funeral than the joy of a wedding. His mention of the plenary indulgence "in the hour of death" sounded as unreal to me as it was familiar to him.

Out of respect for convention, the object, which became the most precious thing in my life, was not exhibited on the billiard table, where a splendid silver tea set gleamed as Pier Giorgio's "official" gift. That green table, chosen by Pier Giorgio a few months later to stretch out his poor limbs wracked with pain, would become the mute witness to the rapid spread of the polio virus.

The crucifix remained in a corner wrapped in the crumpled newspaper. In 1939 it became the only object saved when we had to leave Warsaw in a hurry.

I, too, had given Pier Giorgio something: a thousand of the three thousand lire I had received from Grandmother Frassati. It was the first thousand lire note he possessed, so while he was waving it under all eyes, in his thoughts he had already given it away. Pier Giorgio did not even want to claim for himself the merit of giving it. He confirmed to me on February 14: "You will receive the letters from the Club and the Conference of St. Vincent, to each of whom I have given five hundred lire in your name."

* * *

How fast the time went before my wedding day on January 24. Pier Giorgio felt that his only "accomplice" was going away for good, and he wrote to me: "This time we will be separated not just for a few days but for our whole life." "I know what it means to be alone at home", he murmured, and, alone, he bore on his shoulders the crumbling structure that was our family.

Coming home punctually for the only two half hours in which he met our parents must have been a burden to him. Sitting between two silences thick with rancor must have been a sacrifice that no day to come could alleviate. He became assiduous in accompanying our father and made every effort to "make up for two".

It was not easy, neither for one nor for two, to be in that atmosphere where our mother's exasperated sensitivity had reached the point of making any relationship impossible. She lived as the sanest person in the world, but we had the deep-rooted conviction that we had wronged her even if we caused her only the slightest upset. Every tiny incident acquired enormous dimensions in that silent, irremediable struggle between our father and mother.

* * *

For the last time, although of course we did not know it then, Pier Giorgio put on society clothes with sighs and groans. He was helped by a maid to straighten his notoriously crooked tie and to insert the pearls in the tiny button holes that drove him mad. For the last time, he put on the stiff, starched shirt. He mumbled that he would give all his clothes to the poor. "But the poor don't need dinner jackets", replied the lady. "Well, I'll sell my clothes and give them the money." Fate mocked his efforts to "make himself look nice" by placing next to him at the wedding dinner a new ugly Polish cousin who spoke French badly and no German. His great sadness was not even relieved by any conversation.

In the small chapel at the archbishop's house, all decked with flowers, I lost Pier Giorgio. The tall figure of Carlo Sforza beside the Marchese Garroni's round one, my witnesses, hid those bright eyes which were surely seeking mine. I did not even realize that my father was deathly pale; he gave the reason to Aunt Elena after Pier Giorgio's death:

> Did I ever tell you about the vision I had at the archbishop's house on the day of Luciana's wedding? Ask Alda. When I went into the hall where the altar stood, in its place I saw a bier, a bier that would destroy everything, how I did not know. I did not see, did not feel, but I understood everything. And for the first time in my life I felt faint: for a second, perhaps less, I lost consciousness.

After the service, the archbishop was concerned only with Pier Giorgio. He knew that he was suffering the loss of my presence in his life.

There are moments in which the human soul, free of all fetters, laid bare, reveals more to others than to itself. On that sad winter afternoon at the railway station, I read in my brother's farewell the signs of his dismay. He trembled all over and his tears fell almost dry from eyes burning with pain. He could not form whole words; they came out with a stammer that almost turned into a scream. I reassured him, telling him we would see each other in a few days, because it was impossible for me to leave Italy with that vision of him.

The next day Pier Giorgio wrote to his closest friend, Marco Beltramo:

Last night the parting was terrible. You can imagine what it was like to see my only sister, the companion of my childhood, leave for such distant shores. It was for me a devastating blow.

Sad that his sister was getting married.

CHAPTER 15

Memories—February 1925

Pier Giorgio could not fail to love the mountains; for him they were an amusement in the Lord, rather than a distraction from the Lord:

> Every day, my love for the mountains grows more and more. If my studies permitted, I'd spend whole days in the mountains contemplating the Creator's greatness in that pure air.

However, although the mountains represented a precious relief in his days packed with other people's miseries, work, and study, he was still able calmly to renounce mountain climbing for Mass or a service such as the Easter Communion of his poor. Many have spoken of his mountains, of whole days passed among the snow-capped peaks, and everyone knows these images of him. The meaning is clear: purification, ascent. Especially because excursions then meant hard work: preparation of the rucksacks, carrying them for long hours, until the meal eaten on the snow, with no sign of a bar or heated room. The only comfort was the little hostel hidden away where one slept bundled up and woke with surprise in the morning to find ice in the bowl.

What Pier Giorgio felt for the mountains he described one day to Tina Ajmone-Catt: "These Alpine climbs have a strange magic in them so that no matter how many times they are repeated and however alike they are, they are never boring, in the same way as the experience of spring is never boring but fills our spirit with gladness and delight."

With simplicity, as always, Pier Giorgio tried to make the Sunday excursions accessible to all, because he knew how damaging the city and idleness are to the young. He encouraged them, saying: "Learn to be stronger in spirit than in your muscles. If you are you will be real apostles of faith in God."

The year that I and others could not be with him, Pier Giorgio took less pleasure in the climb and in getting over the difficult passes. I could not go because I was too busy. I watched him departing with a rope hidden in his bag so as not to worry our mother. And I watched him return with only one ski, because he had lost another in a storm. He still had the Scottish beret I had bought him in London.

The third-class carriages in which he traveled were full of joy. "I travel third because there isn't a fourth", Pier Giorgio answered those who were surprised at his uncomfortable choice—loaded down with skis, sweaters, resounding with songs and anxious queries about the only unknown: the snow. The skiers were a family, and, if some of them had their differences in the city, in the mountains they were all united in a single grand passion.

To my amazement, Pier Giorgio always obstinately chose to be with the ugliest person in the group, the poorest and most out of place. What madness was this? I asked myself. Pier Giorgio, who shared my blood, Pier Giorgio who loved our mother so much that he imitated her in many things, might have used her standards in choosing his companions. In reality, he was the support of so many discouraged people and the prop of weak consciences.

He admired my character, even though it was not always

tempered with charity and faith. I could not resign myself to the way his friends continually took advantage of Pier Giorgio because of his father's position. "Oh, Pier Giorgio," they said to him one day, showing him a newspaper with a tone of envy mixed with pleasure, "while you are here your father is with the King." Without the slightest curiosity about the report in *La Stampa*, or any embarrassment, he replied: "But I am a peasant, and I am here."

Humble

It sometimes happened that my behavior contradicted his plans and disappointed his wishes. No one ever saw him more gloomy than at Sauze, when, perhaps, wanting to show him that—given the circumstances—missing Mass was not very serious, I hurriedly set out for the Capanna Kind, thus rendering useless his usual effort to gather all punctually in the little church. His work of months and months, getting up in the morning to "skim" the lazy and the late, his harshness toward himself, everything seemed to crumble in the face of my attitude. Another day he welcomed me in a very bad mood because instead of looking after a less able friend, who was continually falling, I had left her behind and skied on to Oulx.

These were old memories because, in that February, I was far away. Pier Giorgio's renunciation of his love was like an indictment of my happiness, and I wanted news of him. I had written to him and marked the envelope "To Pier Giorgio. Personal". This was unusual, no matter how confidential the subject.

> I have not got my pen and so I don't know how I will write to you. But first I want to thank you so much for your nice letter. Dear little brother, your phrase "separated for life" caused me so much pain. But it is not really so and will not be, only a brief separation which will make us love and understand each other all the more.

Won't it? So don't forget, Giorgio, to write everything
you think, if you are happy or sad. You know and you too
feel that lately we have come closer, so, Giorgio, give your
sister this great pleasure of not letting her feel that this
short absence can ever make us grow apart. I say short
because I count on seeing you soon, you know, little
brother? . . . Goodbye, Giorgio. I send you a big, big hug,
and again I beg you to write me *everything* you are thinking. Do you promise? A big kiss . . .

And he wrote to me:

February 14, 1925

You ask me if I am happy. How can I not be? As long as
faith gives me strength I am happy. Any Catholic can't
help but be happy. Sadness should be banned from Catholic souls. Pain is not sadness, which is a disease worse than
any other. This disease is nearly always caused by atheism,
but the end we are created for shows us the way, which
may be full of thorns but is not sad. It is happy even
through pain. And in these days I rejoice and am cheerful
because Marco Beltramo has come from Livorno.

So they were together for the last carnival. They wore old
bowler hats and walked about the Via Roma. Then, in the
same headgear, they went out in the snow, lodging in the
Cesana inn, in the small freezing room my brother chose to
occupy, giving others his heated one.

* * *

On his last climb to the Lunelle, he did not go with Marco
Beltramo but Guido Unterrichter, who later recalled it with
some emotion:

It was Sunday, June 7, 1925. Pier Giorgio arrived at the
railway station of Lanzo by public transport a few minutes
before the train left. He had overslept and so had had to

attend Mass half an hour later than he had meant to. He was happy and in a good mood, as ever. When we arrived at Pessinetto station we began at once to make for our goal, the Lanzo Lunelle. Pier Giorgio had to guide us until [we reached] the "via accademica" because Pol and I did not know the area.

A little beyond the last cottages we found a beautiful rhododendron bush. Pier Giorgio decided to take it home and so we left it intact. We dug it up on our way back. A little farther up there was a small hill from which, according to Pier Giorgio, the peak of the Lunelle could be seen and the crest we wanted to follow. But when we got there we could not see our peak. Farther up there was another pass. Pier Giorgio guaranteed that this was the pass we had to reach. But we were beginning to have doubts, and unkind remarks as to the authenticity of the peak were to be heard. We climbed on cheerfully with much teasing. Pier Giorgio took it in good part and even enjoyed our jokes. Meanwhile, the weather had turned bad; it began to rain. But the spring beauty of the hill country was nonetheless impressive. Pier Giorgio enjoyed it with great enthusiasm. Everything was in flower and from the hill came gusts of perfumed air from a great spread of little red flowers carpeting the ground. When we reached the pass our worst fears came true. We could not see the peak or the crest of the Lunelle! A cowherd told us we had missed our way. We went down and began climbing in the right direction. We stopped to eat at a spring and continued until we reached the rock. The weather had improved. If I am not mistaken, Pier Giorgio was second on our rope, and he helped me at the difficult places. I remember how he thoroughly enjoyed the climbing, and he particularly liked some double-roped descents necessary to get over the spurs of the crest in certain places. Then we reached the last difficult leg, the "placca Santi", where Cesarino Rovere, a first-year student at the Polytechnic, had died in 1921. As I did not have suitable shoes, we were forced to go the normal way. As soon as we reached the top—we continued alone—he told us to recite a *De Profundis* together for Cesarino Rovere. Pier Giorgio's kind and good thought impressed me deeply, and I decided to follow his example. The next time I get to some peak I will pray for those who died on that mountain. A little less than two months from that day I was in the mountains again in the Trentino, on a beautiful peak, but which did not yet have any dead. I recited the *De Profundis* for Pier Giorgio. And so every time I am up in the mountains and pray, I remember vividly who taught me this, the kindest and most gentle act a mountaineer can perform for his fallen brother.

We returned to our packs and began the descent through a magnificent expanse of rhododendrons in flower. While he was picking some, Pier Giorgio said: "If only Mama were here to see these colors!" At the spring where we had stopped in the morning, we ate a little. Pier Giorgio gave us *Pfefferkuchen* [spiced cookies]. When we arrived at the railway station he offered us a bottle of wine. On the train coming home, we met other climbers whom we knew. We entered Turin singing. I remember that Pier Giorgio sang with real enthusiasm; he felt the song's beauty, and he could not resist his desire to join in, even with his voice. In the city, children seeing us laden with rhododendrons came and asked us for one. Pier Giorgio, with his usual kindness, stopped at once, gave them what they asked for, and enjoyed seeing them go away happy. . . .

My brother wrote about this hike to Marco Beltramo on June 22:

If the Sunday trip had been completed, it would have been a victory because we would have baptized a new route. In fact, from researches made, it appears that no one has ever been up it, only down. At any rate we shall return some Sunday armed with some pegs, and if we have the honor of first ascent, we could call it "Sinister Ones" Route or something. Thank you for your card and for prayers promised. I am most grateful for these because they are better than anything else, especially for someone who is taking a serious step.

Prayer

CHAPTER 16

Charity

Blessed are the merciful

I have a special predilection for the apostolate of charity.

St. Paul was Pier Giorgio's main moral nourishment, the principal source of his religious thinking. At home, nobody remembered Paul. We just knew about the road to Damascus and a sudden conversion and that was it. Pier Giorgio, on the other hand, wrote:

> The mind sated with arid science sometimes finds peace and refreshment and spiritual enjoyment in the reading of St. Paul. I'd like you to try to read St. Paul. It is wonderful and the spirit is cheered and ennobled by reading him. It spurs us on to follow the right way and return to it whenever we leave it through sin.

He had got hold of the Epistles translated by Ramorino. (Pier Giorgio copied by hand the Hymn to Charity in order always to have it at hand.) He read them on the tram or in the street, and, to anyone who wanted to know what was in the book, he said, "words of eternal life". The family knew almost nothing about his secret wisdom. He read St. Augustine, and some of the writings of St. Thomas Aquinas, whose *Summa Theologica* he was beginning to study. His favorite Gospel was Matthew's because of the Sermon on the Mount. His favorite theme was that of the encyclical *Rerum Novarum*.

He knew Pope Innocent III's *De Contemptu Mundi* and shared its contempt for riches and its love of the poor. He knew Veuillot's Testament by heart. He was enthusiastic about the Psalms. He also read Heine and Goethe to enrich his spiritual gifts.

His personality was continually growing in depth and breadth, refined by the pain of renunciation and a remarkable presentiment of death. A year before, he had taken out a Club Alpino insurance policy (number 695) benefiting me in the sum of 25,000 lire if he had an accident in the mountains. He had thought of me, as that last July he thought of his poor. He included me among his favorites and made me his heir with them.

He loved the poor with Christ's eyes and tried all he could to make other young people share his passion:

> Every one of you [we read in his notes on a speech about charity] knows that the foundation of our religion is charity. Without it all our religion would crumble, because we would not really be Catholics as long as we did not carry out or rather shape our whole lives by the two commandments in which the essence of the Catholic faith lies: to love God with all our strength and to love our neighbor as ourselves. And here is the explicit proof that the Catholic faith is based on real love and not, as so many would like in order to quiet their consciences, on violence.
>
> With violence, hatred is sown and then its evil fruits are gathered. With charity we sow peace among people, but not the peace of the world, true peace which only faith in Jesus Christ can give us by making us brothers and sisters.
>
> I know this way is steep and difficult and full of thorns, whereas the other at first sight looks easier and more pleasant and satisfying. But if we look at those who

unfortunately follow the wicked ways of the world, we see that they never have in them the serenity that comes from facing a thousand difficulties and renouncing material pleasure to follow God's law.

Today, after a terrible war that has affected the whole world, bringing material and moral ruin, we have a strict duty to cooperate in the world's moral regeneration so that a radiant dawn may break in which all nations recognize Jesus Christ as King—not only in words but in all their people's lives, as the Florentine Republic did in the Middle Ages. But to complete this enterprise, it is necessary to work enormously hard. One of the most appropriate tasks is that offered by the Conferences of St. Vincent.

This simple institution is suitable for students because it does not involve commitment apart from being in a particular place one day a week and then visiting two or three families every week. You will quickly see how much good we can do to those we visit and how much good we can do to ourselves.

The members who visit these families are, I would say, unworthy instruments of Divine Providence. As we grow close to the poor, bit by bit we gain their confidence and can advise them in the most terrible moments of this earthly pilgrimage. We can give them the comforting words of faith, and we often succeed, not by our own merit, in putting on the right road people who have strayed without meaning to.

I think I can say that the Conference of St. Vincent, with its visits to the poor, serves to curb our passions. It gives us incentives to get on the right road, by which we are all trying to reach the great gate.

Seeing daily the faith with which families often bear the most atrocious sufferings, and their constant sacrifices, and seeing that they do all this for the love of God, often makes us ask why I, who have had so many things from

God, have always been so neglectful, so bad, while they, who have not been privileged like me, are infinitely better than I. Then we resolve in our conscience to follow the way of the cross from then onward, the only way that leads us to eternal salvation.

Many knew Pier Giorgio's charity well, and his works were noted by Angiolo Gambaro in his diary while Pier Giorgio was alive:

In my limited everyday life I have never received such a deep impression as that from the strong personality of this young man.

I think that the model of virtue offered to us by Pier Giorgio is a great thing. He goes about in silence and in secret, without applause, and to the poor he gives bread and his heart, to the orphan an affectionate caress, to the old his luminous smile, to the sick the balm of his loving care. There is heroism in his apostolate. He almost deserts the family in which he could have all the chances, the satisfaction of all pleasures, and it is in the hard school of this world that he forges a strong soul, with constancy, energy, courage, sacrifice, all that is beautiful, worthy, glorious. He ignores the brilliant possibilities that a high income would allow him and is not afraid to carry his singular evangelical spirit of renunciation, detachment, and poverty into a life which we humans have turned into a wild party where rude guests each grab the food from their neighbors instead of offering it around.

One cannot fail to be moved by his generous work, his warm, pure faith, his modesty and constant good temper. This evening when I was in contact with his ardent and communicative zeal for Christian works, I was deeply moved.

Carlo Florio, a fellow member, describes the spirit with which Pier Giorgio approached the poor:

I attended the Conferences of St. Vincent more from family tradition than conviction. Pier Giorgio must have understood, because it was he who taught me how to do works of charity. It is true that I did not hide anything of my perplexity from him. I asked him, for example, how one could manage to enter certain houses cheerfully where the first welcome was a nauseating smell. I asked him, "How do you manage to overcome your revulsion?" He answered me: "Don't ever forget that even though the house is sordid, you are approaching Christ. Remember what the Lord said: the good you do to the poor is good done to me." And he continued: "Around the sick, the poor, the unfortunate, I see a particular light, a light that we do not have."

CHAPTER 17

Frugality and Faith

Blessed are the poor in spirit

I beg you to pray for me a little, so that God may give me an iron will that does not bend and does not fail in his projects.

Gathered in the Cenacolo, the FUCI members, at the invitation of Monsignor Pini, recited three Hail Marys for the one who would die first among them. Pier Giorgio was with them.

My brother turned twenty-four on April 6. I, who received a monthly allowance from my father, had frequently protested that Pier Giorgio, a student engineer, received nothing. Our father decided to give him five thousand lire. This was a very significant sum at the time. Pier Giorgio certainly had no trouble in knowing how to use the money: "I have a bank that gives a thousand percent", he said one day, while he was going with Pietro Occelli to the slums of Madonna della Pace. In his heart, he had immediately decided to give the money for equipment for the St. Vincent Conference at the Milites Mariae Circle.

With regard to money, he considered himself to be the administrator of a treasure that did not belong to him, of which he would have to give an account one day. That is why he could not bear avarice or waste. He reprimanded the

144

servants because they did not gather up scraps of bread, and he spent time gathering the leftovers even after a picnic in the mountains. He knew the effort necessary to scrape together the few lire that his charity transformed into medicines, books, shoes, bread, wood, and coal. He saved ruthlessly, but only and always for the benefit of others. To this end he set his will to make a continual effort.

He had willpower for himself and others. He only had to exchange a few words to win a friend, whom he then looked after and advised. His whole life was characterized by numerous intense human relationships, and they consumed so much of his energy that he said: "I feel like someone who is drowning and has to find the strength for one more stroke." So frequently he asked for prayers to help him strengthen "that will which becomes virtue when it succeeds in mastering itself". One had only to look at him to realize how easily temptations might come to him.

He was dark, a bit above average height, with large shoulders and robust arms. His untidy hair met his forehead in a harmonious line with quite a low midpoint. His eyebrows were not too thick, and perfectly shaped. They framed large, black eyes, full of expression, accentuated by very long curly lashes. He had an aquiline nose, a regular mouth that stood out in his tanned face, very white teeth, and small, well-placed ears.

His good looks, social position, and wonderful health, which might have been stumbling blocks for others, were steps for climbing higher for Pier Giorgio.

He continued to live spartanly in his freezing room, which was never heated, with barely enough blankets. His manly approach to life made his engagement in the struggle for himself and others easier. He was especially close to our mother and had decided to sacrifice everything just to help her. His letters reveal his intention of sharing everything beautiful with her, while hiding or making little of failures. In short, he wanted to create a serene world around her to console her for her difficult life.

Not wanting to leave her, after he had been up the San Mauro hill for what would be the last time to find silence in the Jesuit retreat house of Santa Croce, he returned to Pollone, where he spent his last Easter. He reentered the large house, which was full of signs of our life together, as I myself was to realize a few months later.

In the garden full of flowers, with his usual joy, he greeted the gardener, who was happy at the presence of his former helper. His sonorous voice was heard again, and the neighbors smiled and said to each other that Pier Giorgio's "sermons" were back.

He went out to accompany the old and almost blind Don Vigliani, who was the assistant parish priest of Pollone. He did not leave him at the door of the house. Instead, he went in, sat him down, went to look for his slippers, then, having checked the hour at which he was to go and serve Mass next day, he said goodbye.

He went to Oropa and prayed for me to his Madonna. He passed Father Rizzi's observatory, assuring him that he would come back soon. He went to the Pollone cemetery to take his flowers and prayers. But already, one could feel a mysterious emptiness descending on the great hall of the Villa Ametis. That Easter, Mama wrote me one of her most heartrending letters:

I am heading toward the realization of that horrible dream, that nightmare in which I wander alone through the rooms and none of those I love are there. This year Pier Giorgio won't be there anymore, my silent son who is the blessing of the house. Granny and he are its cornerstones.

She certainly did not imagine that her Easter boy was hearing for the last time the bells announcing the glory that had welcomed him into the world.

* * *

"The life of the good is the most difficult, but it is the quickest to get to heaven", Pier Giorgio said to Ester Pignata. Ester had been a maid in the house for a few months when, sad and disheartened, she started to praise the lure of a care-free life. Ester had opened the door to Pier Giorgio's poor so many times that she had received their homage of flowers on St. George's day [the poor left flowers for Pier Giorgio on what they thought was his name day]. She had patiently learned from him how to answer the telephone, and, enflamed by Pier Giorgio's example, she had started going to Mass, following the ritual with a book given to her by Pier Giorgio and dedicated: "In prayer the soul rises above life's sadnesses."

Pier Giorgio wanted to give his faith to all. The faith flowed from his profound conviction that faith was a vital necessity before being a duty. His faith was filled with the spirit of sacrifice and forgiveness. He wished that everybody would actively adhere to the precepts of the gospel.

Pier Giorgio was only strict in judging certain people who were ostentatiously pious but indulged in reproachable behavior. Rather than their frequent Communions, he would have preferred that such people not profane the church. He thought that religion, being love, should exclude everything that smacked of mere duty. He did not view Communion as an obligation, and the day he heard someone he admired saying: "Tomorrow I have to go to Communion", he was pained by it as by a lack of respect toward God.

He never preached to me. And in that moment when I rushed back to Turin from Holland because our grandmother was ill, there was no time for sermons. But I noticed that something strange had happened in him, something that overcame the sorrow I felt for the coming loss of Grandmother Linda Ametis. In fact, the slow decline of a life that was almost ninety years long seemed natural to us all, and even more so to my brother.

By this time, my father wanted a legal separation, and my mother was tormented by the humiliating prospect. On May 7, with Pier Giorgio motionless at the San Filippo altar rails, she had snapped at cousin Rina Maria Pierazzi, who asked her for news of Grandmother Linda: "It would be better if we all died!" But, with Grandmother, only one died, for all.

* * *

"Faith enables us to bear the thorns with which our life is woven." These words of Pier Giorgio's are from a note dated "Turin, 5/3/1925" to Clementina Luotto, whose mother was ill.

For years, Pier Giorgio had been able to transcend the things of this world, thanks to his clear intuition of the essence of goodness. He was a man of unbending integrity, without false modesty, without hidden cowardice. He fixed his eyes on the person speaking to him, man or woman. He used his physical and spiritual gifts only to persuade others to virtue. He persuaded Ester. He persuaded the midwife friend of Bonini, when he explained to her that there exists a Person infinitely superior to all the things of the world. He persuaded Signorina Rigo, deserting a party so as not to leave her alone at night. He persuaded Father Righini, who asked him to see Elisa Reineri home after a nighttime Adoration. She felt the need to thank him for having chosen "not a young man but an angel". He convinced Signorina Emilia Bertola, to whose apologies for having made him wait, and having therefore made him arrive breathless for the train, he replied: "To get into Paradise I would have had to wait longer", and "let's hope I arrive in time, as we did just now." He convinced Signorina Ajmone-Catt of the beauty of death, of the power of his rosary, showing it to her with the words: "I always carry my will in my pocket."

Through Pier Giorgio, many gained the certainty of tran-scendence. And when he died, and they all scattered, each one bore his mark and a feeling of regret.

CHAPTER 18

Final Days—June 1925

Blessed are those who are persecuted

I am waiting day after day to arm myself with good will to pursue my final task to the end, for I am close to harvesting what I have sown. Unfortunately, the days go by one after the other and instead of finding some improvement in myself, I perceive that it is the beast which wins in the struggle with the spirit. Only in the prayers of my friends do I see a powerful help.

Thus Pier Giorgio wrote on June 15. Nineteen days later, death, which he had always looked in the face, welcomed him into its peace. It was his last month on earth, even though his family did not grasp this reality.

We were accustomed to the atmosphere of the house, but I had been living a different life, full of surprises, whereas Pier Giorgio had been wrapped up in books and exams. He made a list of these on June 27, as if to leave the only account of his life that meant anything to us. As he had completed twenty exams, there were two blank spaces: the ones he still had to take to get his coveted degree in engineering and to put that degree to the service of those he judged to be among the most unhappy workers. This degree was intended to hide his missionary vocation from the eyes of the household. But the title of engineer, so near at hand, would have been treated by our parents as a piece of paper, perhaps necessary, but nothing more than that. A few months before, he had written: "I am so happy to finish my studies in such a beautiful year [the Holy Year]."

Our parents knew he was always going to church and the Club and that he had a lot of friends who were priests. They knew he did not allow himself any other enjoyments, except the odd game of billiards at the Cesare Balbo with the pool for the benefit of the Club. His interest in these types of activities had been ascribed by them to his low intelligence, and they did not want to look into it more deeply. Maybe he sold Catholic papers, took part in so many Conferences of St. Vincent, and went to Communion every day, but at the appropriate moment, Papa, with his authority, would be expecting him. His career had already been chosen. In the administrative office of *La Stampa*, his chair, table, and account books were already waiting for him. The lawyer Garino, an old friend of the family, left Fiat to introduce Pier Giorgio to the job.

My father had never uttered a word to my brother about such an important decision. He had never held a conversation about his son's aspirations, as if Pier Giorgio were a thing with which he could do as he liked—as if his degree, his plans for other degrees, and work in mining were a joke, and all his hard work and hopes deserving merely a smile.

Our father was not used to inquiring how others felt, and, in this case, as he was afraid of looking his son in the eye, he asked his friend Cassone, a chronicler from *La Stampa*, to pass on the verdict to the already sacrificed victim. Cassone, of whom we were so fond, choked when he heard Pier Giorgio asking, with tears in his eyes: "Do you think all this will please Papa?" Cassone nodded, and Pier Giorgio said: "Well, tell him I accept."

He had simply deferred the moment in which he would leave Father and Mother, aware that his first duty was not to desert the post in which God had put him: the small trench in which he defended their so-called conjugal unity. With the same submission with which he had renounced his first love, he surrendered again. After his painful confession the previous December of his love for and sacrifice of Laura Hidalgo, he had said: "Certainly I would have liked to be a missionary, but now you are leaving." That desolate "would have" contains the secret of my beloved brother's life.

The prospect of joining *La Stampa* was an even more painful one: the renunciation of his apostolate among the miners was the harbinger of his death agony. He agreed to look after money that was not his, money that had always been an enemy to him, only in order to defend our mother.

My marriage had brought the situation to a head and had left Pier Giorgio as a pawn in a tragic game. On the day I had confessed to Mama in Berlin that I had fallen in love with an Italian officer, she had protested: "If you marry Lazzarini, you will be responsible for our separation." These were harsh words to say to an eighteen-year-old, but they were true. And our father used our mother's hypersensitivity as another argument to prevent Pier Giorgio from doing what he wanted. Our father built up his arguments to dissuade Pier Giorgio from his vocation by predicting that he would become a fanatic, useless at *La Stampa* and to his family if he were to continue frequenting religious organizations.

No one at home would ever have tolerated his becoming a missionary.

"The Lord's will was not that", he replied one day to Enrico Lanfranco, who asked him why he had not become a priest.

So he agreed. He accepted God's final offer and death

decided. Pier Giorgio had served and loved him without stint. Poliomyelitis came quickly and inexorably. Pier Giorgio carried with him the secret of his ruined household, the sacrifice he had made to cement the crumbling structure. He was not being rhetorical when he asked: "Why create one family in order to destroy another?"

The terrible disease was the end for a body already weak because its soul was consumed with pain. Everyone noted that his jacket was getting too big and was not suitable for Frassati's son: "He seemed to be dancing inside it", declared the cook who saw him during those days. And father: "I saw you with a friend. You looked like a scarecrow compared to him. How can you go about in such a state?" We knew our father. He had never bothered much about elegance himself, and, this time, his words were intended as yet another criticism of our mother. Pier Giorgio replied: "But Beltramo is wearing a uniform!"

In fact it was his poor shoulders, which I saw one day when he was taking off his jacket, that made him look so different. To my mind, he looked stooped, but I attributed that wasting away to the hard toil he put in to get through the exams. In fact, death had already put its mark on him. Everything had to be wiped out: memories, hopes, images. Having lived his whole life in Jesus Christ, he was now able to attribute to renunciation and suffering a creative value: "Human sorrows affect us but if they are seen in the light of religion, and thus of resignation, they are not harmful, but healthy, because they purify the soul of the small and inevitable stains with which we mortals with our most imperfect nature so often mark it."

CHAPTER 19

Death—July 1925

Do not be worried, for the life of the good is very short.

These are the words that Pier Giorgio had used a little earlier to console his friend Mario Ghemlera on the death of his sister. He had also helped him with the funeral expenses. Pier Giorgio also expressed his hope to our driver, Italo Pavoni: "I'd like to be old so that I could go to heaven quicker." "And what will the Sinister Ones do without Robespierre?" Pavoni had asked. "I will wait for them all in heaven", was the reply. In his study, everything had been tidied up: on the table there was a letter dated July 1 with one of the habitual requests for a recommendation that he had to do for some needy person or a friend. Pier Giorgio was ill. He had terrible pains in his back, and he had to get up and go to meet death in another room. He had to recite the prayers for the dying for our grandmother when he himself was dying.

"If it was a question of money, no one would die in this house", he had replied a few days earlier to Elisabetta Musso. But it was a question of heart, and Pier Giorgio was dying. He died, misunderstood to the end, leaving a stupendous legacy: "Better to go to heaven than to live down here, because things are too bad here. Let us do good to one another while we have time", he had said the Sunday before to Brother Giuseppe of the Missions.

misunderstood
(by family)

Now that all his great sacrifices were ending in death, Pier Giorgio knew they had been in vain, that our father and mother were going to part.

* * *

At the end of the week, his life was complete.[1] He died on Saturday, July 4, 1925, just as the exams were finishing. He encountered "the most beautiful day of his life" in Turin, in whose schools, streets, and piazzas he had unhesitatingly practiced his religion and charity. He died from an incurable disease; a children's disease destroyed his strong, solid frame. Poliomyelitis is contagious, but strangely, it left those around him untouched.

His last days were sheer physical and moral torment, but he was too humble and self-denying to mind the indifference of others. No one took any notice of him. Even I, although I had some intuition, was certainly not aware: "Pier Giorgio is vomiting and has a temperature," I told our mother, who had always said that these two symptoms together are alarming. But Mama was overwhelmed by our grandmother's dying. *mother did not care for him*

Pier Giorgio's final walk to the nearby parish church had been to call a priest to bless our dying grandmother. But when they gave her Extreme Unction he was not told. He heard about it when it was over and burst into tears because he had been excluded at such a moment. He leaned against the doorpost and could not calm down. Then he went to bed.

After spending the whole day alone, he was called to Grandmother Linda's bedside. He was in pajamas with a blanket around his hips. He suddenly seemed even thinner and to be in pain. Grandmother died that evening, Wednesday, July 1. Pier Giorgio had a deep affection for her, even though she

---

[1] *Una vita mai spenta* (4th rev. ed. [Turin: La Stampa, 1992]), gives an account of Pier Giorgio's suffering and heroic resignation.

had lost her memory years before and was a shadow of her former self.

Although he was ill, cruel and unjust reproaches were still his lot: "It seems impossible that whenever you are needed you are never there", our mother said to him about Grandmother's coming funeral. She did not know that Pier Giorgio had fallen down three times to go to pray in her room, and that he had been able to get up again only by clinging to the corridor wall and had spent the whole night stretched out on the billiard table. Pier Giorgio could not rest. As usual, he put up with our mother's nervousness in silence, and returned to his room, leaving the bed beside our mother's in which a few hours earlier he had taken refuge in a desperate attempt to find protection.

His minutes were numbered. It was only by chance that he did not remain alone on his last night but one. Cousin Mario Gambetta was able to hear Pier Giorgio's last words, but, although he had known him since childhood and was like a brother to him, he did not realize that Pier Giorgio was dying. Everything went unnoticed. Everything was carefully suppressed by Pier Giorgio so as "not to disturb"! Even the suspicion Mario had at a certain moment was dissolved by the heroism of a joke and a smile. Pier Giorgio went alone with his sad joy "to his true country to sing God's praises".

On Friday morning, leaving for the funeral at Pollone, I said goodbye to him as one would to someone whom one will see again soon. Pier Giorgio was already paralyzed below the waist and no one in the house knew it. I left Turin with our aunt. Our father had reached Pollone the evening before, and our mother had decided at the last moment, "only" because of her extreme tiredness, to stay in the house and "meanwhile" keep Pier Giorgio company instead of the usual friend Alda, who came with us to the funeral.

"Pier Giorgio could choose a better moment to be ill",
was Mama's greeting to Marco Beltramo, who had come to
visit his Robespierre.

Within a few hours I no longer found the Pier Giorgio I
knew, the Pier Giorgio who had been with me all my life.

* * *

They were putting Grandmother's coffin in the grave when
an unexpected telephone call from Turin hastened the sad
ceremony. None of us present in the Pollone cemetery could
imagine that, three days later, we would be burying Pier
Giorgio beside his grandmother.

At that time, our anxiety was for our father, always in the
limelight because of *La Stampa*. We all thought the call was
for political reasons, certainly not about Pier Giorgio. Rushing to Turin, disaster was far from our minds, and I talked of
leaving at once to rejoin my husband, whom I had left for
more than a month at The Hague. Professor Micheli's car in
front of our house was the first sign, which was immediately
confirmed by Mama: "Pier Giorgio is ill, very ill!"

I had no time to tidy myself as Pier Giorgio was already
calling me. So as not to show my dismay, I ran first into his
study to fetch the Alpaca jacket he had asked for and from
which he drew, in my presence, a pawn ticket from the
Monte di Pietà and a small box of injections. He insisted on
writing the note himself and asked that it be sent to Giuseppe
Grimaldi, a friend of the conference:

> The injections are for Converso and the pawn ticket
> belongs to Sappa: I had forgotten it. Please renew it on
> my account.

It was Friday, the time for visiting the poor. The hour
when Turin saw him with a companion, usually with rosary
in hand, hurrying toward the poor streets. The note was

delivered immediately, and it dismayed the Club and the Conferences of St. Vincent and, gradually, the halls of the Polytechnic, the suburbs, the convents.

The news reached the house of "his" archbishop, who, even though he was engaged on an important duty, when informed by the faithful Francesco, left everything to go to his young friend. But our mother forbade even the archbishop to come near him, for fear of contagion.

Poor Giorgio! Nothing was spared him. In the morning he had to confess and take Communion from Don Formica, the only priest with whom he had once had serious disagreements. From that moment, all means were tried to save him.

The most famous doctors in Turin shook their heads, and, as fate would have it, the generous Arturo Ferrarin could not take off for Paris to fetch anti-polio serum because of a storm. Professor Pescarolo did not give up hope but recommended that the sick man should be left in peace. Thus the task of keeping watch during his last night was entrusted to strangers. Only the hands of Sister Michelina helped him to make his last sign of the cross, and it was her affectionate words that tried to calm his anguished question: "Will God forgive me? Will God forgive me?" Then, at four in the morning, he was given Extreme Unction.

* * *

Sofia Stampini came, all unaware, believing she could give him the vouchers he was always desperate to get hold of. Brother Foi, the Conference porter, came, thunderstruck by the news. Father Ibertis, O.P., came, and he, too, had to respect my mother's strict order to go away. He returned to San Domenico without being able to bless his Fra Gerolamo for the last time.

Cardinal Gamba, in order to be near Pier Giorgio in some

way or other, took the relic of the Blessed Cafasso and sent it to him, while Carlo Borgatello, the Cesare Balbo priest, joined the Fucini's invitation to general prayer. "It was one of the most fervent services I have ever attended", said Don Carlo. At the end, all had misty eyes.

Already, many people in Turin were beginning to understand what his absence meant and tried to arrest the verdict by prayer. But when the Hour of Adoration offered for his life was over, it was known that Pier Giorgio was no more. Beside the couch, the last book my brother had tried to read lay open: the life of St. Catherine of Siena,[2] the saint he loved and envied because she had spoken to Jesus while she was alive.

From Cossila, Grandmother Frassati had written Pier Giorgio a letter that seems to indicate a presentiment in its unusual greeting:

> Your name-day, St. Peter's, is coming, and I am writing to wish you all good things and happiness, and I will pray on this day that your saint may watch over you and guide you always on the right path, which you have always kept to.
>
> I hope to see you soon at Cossila. Papa told me you had only one more exam to go through. You will get your degree immediately after the exams, and so you can rest a bit and make a little journey to The Hague with Luciana for a few days, or somewhere else. . . . I send greetings to all embracing you again in God.

And the foreboding became mysterious knowledge, although no one knew anything about it at the time. On Sunday, July 5, Grandmother Frassati jumped up crying: "Pier Giorgio is calling me, Pier Giorgio is calling me!"

While he was dying, the maid, Ester Pignata, whom he

---

[2] It was the book he had given me when I graduated, with the wish that it might guide me in the ascent toward spiritual perfection.

had taught to believe, wrote on the kitchen calendar: "7 P.M., an irreparable tragedy has occurred. Poor Pier Giorgio. He was a saint and God wanted him with himself!" And the M.P. Spartaco Fazzari, father's friend, with a hand accustomed to noting very different events, wrote in his elegant diary for July 4: "The best man in the world is dead!"

* * *

At home we realized for the first time that something unalterable had happened, too big for us to understand. Meanwhile, the doors began to open to let in new faces, unknown to us as was his life. Mama tried to stop it, not realizing that the revelation of her son's greatness was beginning. At my request, she withdrew the order. The throng of silent people, their faces blank or wet with tears, went in to him, touched him like a relic in front of us who had ignored him for years. It was from these unknown people that we received our greatest lesson.

The crowd continued to pour in until the moment when Pier Giorgio crossed the threshold for the last time through two lines of kneeling people. Thus, all at once, in the streets, on the pavements, from windows, the light of Pier Giorgio shone in the victory of his humility. A dead man was speaking as a holy image can speak when carried in procession. I felt the crumbling of so many hopes. I could not imagine life without my brother. I followed him, lost, while from the undecked coffin he was telling us all that his friends were indeed these poor people, faithful and despairing, who were accompanying him for the last time. A blind man wanted to touch the coffin, another struggled to approach his benefactor. The crowd pressed around his mortal remains. Some wept, some prayed, while that coffin, without a single flower, seemed to rock above a tide of heads. Antonio Cajrola noted a large, middle-aged man whose face was furrowed with tears. It was Giovanni Amendola, an eminent Socialist politician, who had probably never met Pier Giorgio.

When the bearers changed, the coffin tilted, and our Giuseppe Cassone remembers the desperate tenderness of our father's gesture to stop it falling. Perhaps it was due to the weak shoulders of the Fucino Francesco Manara, great-hearted but already suffering from the terminal illness that killed him. A few months later, as he lay on his own death-bed, his friends noticed on Manara's black coat the marks of Pier Giorgio's coffin.

> I'd like to say [writes Ubaldo Leva, a *La Stampa* journalist] that this was the most moving and edifying funeral I have ever been to, either as a journalist or as a private person; not the most solemn, not official, but the most vivid, the warmest, and most human—I mean the most beautiful. Even now, so long afterward, the memory of it makes me feel an amazed tenderness.
>
> I remember that while I was writing my account in haste, I kept choking with emotion as I relived those moments and also because I could not express myself as I should have liked to. . . . I would have liked to speak worthily of the crowd pressing around Pier Giorgio's mortal remains. Nearly all common people, little people, little women and artisans, and lots of mothers with babies. The houses in Borgo Crocetta were emptied of all who were not at work. There were also those who came from other parts of the city. The church was packed, and there were swarms of people outside. Few had known Pier Giorgio but they had heard of his faith, his works of charity, and they had come full of respect and admiration and from curiosity. They wanted to know more, they wanted to know everything about him, the young man who in death had become the friend, the brother, of each of them.

Had to die to be understood

In all this there was something unique, something of a mystery. Everything could have been explained if this had been a famous person, an important life ended. But this was only a young man—a student! His life was just beginning. He had given very little of himself as yet.

This funeral was therefore the first witness, the first consecration of the great soul, the pure spirit of Pier Giorgio. There, it can be said, the canonization process began.

Amid sorrow and dismay, the tears of Father Righini, the exaltation of Father Ibertis, O.P., the sobs of Signora Converso (from a family he attended and for whom he sent the injections the day before his death), Albertini Luigi's embrace of our father,[3] the handkerchiefs, the rosaries, the crowds of poor people come to watch the coffin go by, I barely realized that a new message was being born.

* * *

Tina Ajmone-Catt wrote to Lea Raiteri on the day of Pier Giorgio's funeral:

Dearest Lea,

Perhaps Sunday's *La Stampa* brought you the sad and painful news of Pier Giorgio's death before this letter reaches you.

The pain we are all feeling is indescribable. No words can fill such an emptiness. Anyone who met him feels his value today and the Christian feelings that were in his heart.

What goodness, delicacy, fineness, kindness in helping the poor who turned to him. Do you remember? How many people came here looking for him, here at the Party? Signora Converso, Bertone's mother, that little

---

[3] Editor-in-chief of the rival daily *Corriere della Sera*.

woman came knocking at his door every day, and he was always ready to open it to her.

Signorina Rigo told me she saw Signora Converso clinging to the church door and crying like a baby. And she is right to cry; he did such a lot for her!

Pier Giorgio had a beautiful soul that loved everything beautiful, everything good, everything holy. He was capable of rising to sublime heights, and the true, living light of faith shone in him, that faith which alone teaches us to love in God, with God, and through God.

He knew how to walk amid this lurid world's mud without getting dirty. In a word, Pier Giorgio was one of the few chosen ones, as the Gospel calls them.

Forgive me, dear Lea, this unburdening of my heart and my meandering letter. But then whom else can I confide in, if not in you, who knew him and were close to him? Do you remember? He was our counsellor, always ready to put in a good word, and to see us in harmony.

Alone within four walls that remind me of so many careless hours of joy, everything seems changed. There is no one at the club now, and it seems deserted.

I have tried to pray, but have not been able to. I began to say a rosary. But when I saw in my hands the beads that Pier Giorgio gave me not very long ago, his words came back into my head: "Keep them in memory of me and if every time you say the rosary you say an extra Hail Mary for me, I'll be very grateful." Those beads are and will be the dearest memento I have of him. . . .

I hope to be able to come to you in August. Then we shall be able to go over things we had in common with the great Friend.

Tina

This letter, written on that same July 6, 1925, by Clementina Luotto to Marco Beltramo, gives an idea of what Pier Giorgio's presence meant:

Marco, it is the first night that Pier Giorgio is out of the house, at least in his *sancta persona*, which yesterday I had the grace of contemplating in a light of indescribable beauty and purity.

I have no one to cry with, and I am thinking of you who were much closer than I was to him in everything.

Beside that bed, which seemed like an altar to me, I felt for the first time, with a dismay I can never express, that death came down from above and he was taken up.

Now I recognize that I was so unworthy to be near that soul; and the thought makes me tremble. I am full of confusion and pain because I think that—seeing me as I really am—Pier Giorgio will have crossed me off his list of friends, as one of the vain and unworthy creatures that he had the misfortune of associating with here below. Or perhaps his charity will be fired with new ardor, and he will take pity on one who has more need?

I cannot pray—I do not say for him, which would sound like madness—that he may help me to deserve to remember him. I think that—as punishment to me—the Gospel threat has come true: "I will strike the shepherd and the sheep will be scattered." It was his goodness that kept us united.

May the Lord take account of the many steps he took to come to me and my mother's, to bring me greetings and his good wishes, his invariably serene words, the light of his kind eyes. They were simple as a child's and deep as a prophet's. Who will wipe away his smile from our memory and who will ever smile at us like that again?

And, Marco, that night in the train between Turin and Oulx, in all that whiteness of snow, the Lord allowed us who were with him to see all the different sides of him: wearing that raincoat, helping the railway men to carry the luggage, and then up and down along the train bogged down by snow and water, quoting his beloved poetry—

Carducci and Marradi—out loud, because he thought no one could hear, and we heard his voice sometimes loud, sometimes soft, and he laughed about it, but we felt that only he could do such a thing, to be like that. Then he came back into the compartment—do you remember?—and they all complained about the loud noise. Then he sat down quietly in his place, which was by my side but beyond the arm rest, and I thought he was asleep. I later realized that he was saying his rosary, his gray rosary, the souvenir he left to each of us and which today is so sacred to me that I would give everything not to lose it.

That night we ate, in fact he insisted that we women should eat so as not to fall ill, but he himself did not touch any food. Neither did you, Marco, and then at dawn in that soft, dreamlike whiteness, both of you in that little church. I remember you around that little altar—you both seemed so strong and good to me.

Now who will go to the mountain again? Oh! his bag! Do you remember that overcoat? On the Mussa Plain, and those minerals he carried—for a microbe of garnet, we said, and he laughed and sparkled with joy. And his whistle to call those who were far away? And his meals? From sweet, to salty, to sour, back to sweet, and on again to salty. And Tina: "But Frassati, you are making us lose our appetites!" And he excused himself as if he were guilty of a great fault and offered us all his good things with that deep voice and large gesture. For us who remember him, this gesture will always seem the very image of cordiality, now gone for good.

And then he did such delicate little kindnesses that he made his strong head sometimes seem dreamy and fragile like a child's. He was grateful to be offered an orange; if he was given a flower, he stored it away carefully. His friends wrote to me this year: "What a pity you are not with us!" and he, not knowing they had written: "You are always with us, even when you are far away!" And he understood everything. Marco, there is such a beautiful thought in that book you gave me, that tells something that was particularly sublime about Pier Giorgio's spirit.

One could reveal any feeling to him—as long as it was sincere—and be sure not to be misunderstood. The only thing he did not understand was deceitfulness.

One could not imagine anyone more sensitive. When we went to Sauze that day and it was snowing, his main worry was his Scottish cap: not to get it wet, not to spoil it, because his sister had given it to him. And do you remember that his hair was all covered in snow and we bound an orange scarf around his head so he looked like a shah? And he laughed. But the cap was warmly tucked away at Oulx, folded neatly in my rucksack, not in his, because in his there were too many tins.

And when we arrived he wanted to share his white wine, and we felt we were the kings of Sauze and everyone else ridiculous compared to us. And to think that we did not even know how to fasten our skis! Oh, the marvelous youthfulness that emanated from him and floated around him, which made us so light-hearted, ready to take a plunge, so free of any mortal hindrance, so close to God who was in him! Who will ever give us this purifying joy again? Who will renew not only under our eyes but in us the miracle of joyful holiness, carefree and fresh and reviving as water from an Alpine spring?

I think that I was close to this miracle of grace and my obtuseness did not make me realize it. Not that I did not see at once that there was something absolutely extraordinary in him. You are my witness and I am not saying anything about him—now that death shows him in the light of the burning bush—that I did not say or we did not say before. But I was not able to ask him for help and I learned nothing. Nothing.

And then I did not understand him. Oh, that evening, Marco, the last evening we were together, and he was already unwell!

That winter, in his new mountain costume, he seemed forged in bronze. Now he looked much smaller, thinner, tired. I thought it was the exams, the summer, but he was already beginning to detach himself from us. "You are pale, Frassati!" "I need the mountains!" he said. Yes, to go up high and not with us!

I can't make peace with it. Everything that seemed like a gift in life now seems like a punishment, a tie holding me to earth. The truth is there, on that bed where there is an effusion of celestial peace.

The moon is shining now, the moon we hoped would shine for us on our climb. And he is no longer with us. It is enough to drive you mad.

Nevertheless, he gives his poor relatives the strength to go on living. He will give us the active love we ought to have, above all because he gave us the priceless gift of his friendship.

Shall we go to him together?

I remember and weep alone. Far from Mother and Paolo, I dare not speak to anyone of my sorrow, because it feels like profaning it and because only Laura, Tina, you and Severi know what we six were and what that community of spirit and joy was like that he created. He led and we followed. Will we know how to go on now that he has left us all to ourselves? We will try, won't we? And we will help each other. Rather, you will help me.

Forgive me, dear Marco, and see I was right to call you my brother. This thunderbolt that strikes our deepest soul makes us realize clearly what our feelings and our duties are.

Let us cling to the cross and love each other in his memory as if and more than if he were still with us.

Perhaps that way we shall see his smile shine among us again. O goodness, you are brighter and warmer than the sun, and you are eternal!

Pope John Paul II
on Pier Giorgio Frassati

Homily on the occasion of the opening of an exhibit on
Pier Giorgio at the Dominican friars in Krakow (March 1997)

Among the many names that I could mention I shall select only two.

The first is that of Don Bosco . . . The second name is that of Pier Giorgio Frassati, a figure nearer to our own age (he died in fact in 1925). He shows us in real life what it really means, for a young layman, to give a concrete answer to the "Come, follow me." Even a rapid glance at his life, consummated in the span of barely twenty-four years, is enough to understand what was the answer that Pier Giorgio gave to Jesus Christ. It was that of a "modern" young man, open to the problems of culture, sport—a tremendous mountaineer—to social questions, to the real values of life. At the same time it was that of a deep believer, nourished on the Gospel message, of a staunch, consistent character, passionately eager to serve brothers and consumed by charity which led him to approach, in an order of absolute precedence, the poor and the sick.

April 13, 1980, to the youth of Turin

Pier Giorgio was a young man of an (overflowing) joy that swept everything along with it, a joy that also overcame so many difficulties in his life because the period of youth is always also a period of trial of strength.

March 15, 1983, inauguration of the
San Lorenzo International Youth Center

It is good that you have placed the famous cross of San Damiano in this church. . . . Together with the memory of the ancient cross of San Damiano and the example of St. Francis, I want to recall to you as an incentive for striving toward high ideals also the figure of a young man who lived in our era, Pier Giorgio Frassati. (He was a "modern" youth open to the problems of culture, sports, to social questions, to the true values of life, and at the same time a profoundly believing man, nourished by the Gospel message, deeply interested in serving his brothers and sisters and consumed in an ardor of charity that drew him close to the poor and the sick.) He lived the Gospel Beatitudes.

Rome, April 12, 1984, homily in the presence of
eighty thousand young people at the Olympic Stadium
on the occasion of the International Jubilee for Athletes

I feel that the Church, no less than your homelands, can count on you! You have models to inspire you. I am thinking, for example, of Pier Giorgio Frassati, who was a modern young man open to the values of sport—he was a skillful mountaineer and able skier—but at the same time he bore a courageous witness of generosity in Christian faith and charity toward others, especially the very poor and the suffering. The Lord called him to himself at only twenty-four years of age, in July 1925, but he is still very much alive among us with his smile and his goodness, inviting his contemporaries to the love of Christ and a virtuous life. After the First World War he wrote the following: "Through charity, peace is sown

among people, not the peace that the world gives but the true peace that only faith in Christ can give us, making us brothers and sisters." These words of his, and his spiritual friendship, I leave with you as a program, so that in every part of the world you too may be messengers of the true peace of Christ!

Angelus at the Marian Shrine of Oropa, Italy, July 16, 1989

To those who are devoted to her, especially young people— like Pier Giorgio Frassati, who used to come up here to give himself to prayer—the Blessed Virgin proposes to be a shelter and a refuge, the heavenly Mother who opens her house to give everyone the invigorating experience of a more profound contact with God.

Dear young people who are listening to me! Like Pier Giorgio, may you also discover the way of the Shrine, in order to undertake a spiritual journey which, under Mary's guidance, brings you closer to Christ. You can then become His witnesses with the conviction and keenness which characterized Pier Giorgio's apostolic activity. You will bear witness to Christ, as he did, especially in the university world, in which there are boys and girls who perhaps have not yet resolved the question of the meaning of their life. By word and example you can show that Christ has the really satisfactory solution for the crucial problems of life.

Dear friends, do not hesitate to come up here in search of light and strength for your journey of faith, and a more firm hope for a courageous and consistent Christian commitment in the world of today. Pier Giorgio Frassati stands before you as an outstanding layman of Catholic Action fully aware of his baptismal commitment to contribute to the Christian animation of his social environment, in complete harmony with the bishops of the Church.

Pollone, July 16, 1989

In the afternoon the Holy Father flew to Pollone, a village near Biella, and prayed in the cemetery at the tomb of the Venerable Pier Giorgio Frassati for twenty minutes. Afterward he addressed the local people:

"I greet the members of the family of Pier Giorgio and especially his sister, Signora Luciana Gawronska Frassati.

"A short while ago I went to the tomb of Pier Giorgio Frassati, your illustrious townsman. . . . I wanted to pay homage to a young man who was able to witness to Christ with singular effectiveness in this century of ours. . . .

"I, too, in my youth, felt the beneficial influence of his example, and, as a student, I was impressed by the force of his Christian testimony.

"I should like to underline particularly his works in the Conference of St. Vincent de Paul, and in Catholic Action, of which he remains one of the most fascinating exponents. The particular clarity of his testimony springs from his radical adherence to Christ, from his transparent fidelity to the Church, from the generosity of his missionary work. He offered to all an example which, even today, has lost nothing of his magnetic attraction. I wish everyone, especially the young, to draw inspiration and encouragement from his short but radiant life of consistent Christian witness."

Beatification: Rome, May 20, 1990

Pope John Paul II's Homily from the Beatification Mass of Blessed Pier Giorgio Frassati, May 20, 1990.

1. "I will ask the Father, and he will send you another Advocate to be with you always, the Spirit of truth" (Jn 14:16).

During the Easter season, as we progressively draw near to Pentecost, these words become more and more timely. They were spoken by Jesus in the Upper Room the day before his Passion, as he took leave of his Apostles. His departure—the departure of the Beloved Master through his death and Resurrection—prepares the way for another Advocate (Jn 16:7). The Paraclete will come; he will come precisely because of Christ's redemptive departure which makes possible and inaugurates God's new merciful presence among people. The Spirit of Truth, whom the world neither sees nor knows, however, makes itself known by the Apostles, because "it remains with them and will be in them" (cf. Jn 14:17). And everyone will become witnesses to this on the day of Pentecost.

2. Pentecost, however, is only the beginning, because the Spirit of Truth comes to remain with the Church for ever (cf. Jn 14:16), endlessly renewing itself in future generations. Therefore the words of the Apostle Peter are addressed not only to the people of his day, but also to all of us and our contemporaries. "Sanctify Christ as Lord in your hearts. Always be ready to give an explanation to anyone who asks you for a reason for your hope" (1 Pet 3:15). In our century, Pier Giorgio Frassati incarnated these words of St. Peter in his own life. The power of the Spirit of Truth, united to Christ, made him a modern witness to the hope which springs from the Gospel and to the grace of salvation which works in human hearts. Thus he became a living witness and courageous defender of this hope in the name of Christian youth of the twentieth century.

3. Faith and charity, the true driving forces of his existence, made him active and diligent in the milieu in which he lived, in his family and school, in the university and society; they transformed him into a joyful, enthusiastic

apostle of Christ, a passionate follower of his message and charity. The secret of his apostolic zeal and holiness is to be sought in the ascetical and spiritual journey which he traveled; in prayer; in persevering adoration, even at night, of the Blessed Sacrament; in his thirst for the Word of God, which he sought in Biblical texts; in the peaceful acceptance of life's difficulties, in family life as well; in chastity lived as a cheerful, uncompromising discipline; in his daily love of silence and life's "ordinariness". It is precisely in these factors that we are given to understand the deep wellspring of his spiritual vitality. Indeed, it is through the Eucharist that Christ communicates his Spirit; it is through listening to the word that the readiness to welcome others grows, and it is also through prayerful abandonment to God's will that life's great decisions mature. Only by adoring God who is present in his or her own heart can the baptized Christian respond to the person who "asks you for a reason for your hope" (1 Pet 3:15). And the young Frassati knew it, felt it, lived it. In his life, faith was fused with charity: firm in faith and active in charity, because without works, faith is dead (cf. James 2:20).

4. Certainly, at a superficial glance, Frassati's life-style, that of a modern young man who was full of life, does not present anything out of the ordinary. This, however, is the originality of his virtue, which invites us to reflect upon it and impels us to imitate it. In him faith and daily events are harmoniously fused, so that adherence to the Gospel is translated into loving care for the poor and the needy in a continual crescendo until the very last days of the sickness which led to his death. His love for beauty and art, his passion for sports and mountains, his attention to society's problems did not inhibit his constant relationship with the Absolute. Entirely immersed in the mystery of God and totally dedicated to the constant service of his neighbor: thus we can sum up his earthly life!

He fulfilled his vocation as a lay Christian in many associative and political involvements in a society in ferment, a society which was indifferent and sometimes even hostile to the Church. In this spirit, Pier Giorgio succeeded in giving new impulse to various Catholic movements, which he enthusiastically joined, but especially to Catholic Action, as well as the Federation of Italian Catholic University Students [FUCI], in which he found the true gymnasium of his Christian training and the right fields of his apostolate. In Catholic Action he joyfully and proudly lived his Christian vocation and strove to love Jesus and to see in him the brothers and sisters whom he met on his way or whom he actively sought in their places of suffering, marginalization, and isolation, in order to help them feel the warmth of his human solidarity and the supernatural comfort of faith in Christ.

He died young, at the end of a short life, but one which was extraordinarily filled with spiritual fruits, setting out for his "true homeland and singing God's praises".

5. Today's celebration invites all of us to receive the mes-

sage which Pier Giorgio Frassati is sending to the men and women of our day, but especially to you young people, who want to make a concrete contribution to the spiritual renewal of our world, which sometimes seems to be falling apart and wasting away because of a lack of ideals. By his example he proclaims that a life lived in Christ's Spirit, the Spirit of the Beatitudes, is "blessed", and that only the person who becomes a "man or woman of the Beatitudes" can succeed in communicating love and peace to others. He repeats that it is really worth giving up everything to serve the Lord. He testifies that holiness is possible for everyone, and that only the revolution of charity can enkindle the hope of a better future in the hearts of people.

6. Yes, "tremendous are the deeds of the Lord! Shout joyfully to God all you on earth" (Ps 66:1–3). The verses of the Psalm resound in this Sunday liturgy as a living echo of young Frassati's soul. Indeed, we all know how much he loved the world God created! "Come and see the works of God" (Ps 65/66:5): this is also an invitation which we receive

from his young soul and which is particularly addressed to young people. Come and see God's "tremendous deeds among men" (ibid.). Tremendous deeds among men and women! Human eyes—young, sensitive eyes—must be able to admire God's work in the external, visible world. The eyes of the spirit must be able to turn from this external, visible world to the inner, invisible one: thus they can reveal to others the realm of the spirit in which the light of the Word that enlightens every person is reflected (cf. Jn 1:9). In this light the Spirit of Truth acts.

7. This is the "inner" person. This is how Pier Giorgio appears to us. Indeed, his entire life seems to sum up Christ's words which we find in John's Gospel: "Whoever loves me will keep my word, and my Father will love him, and we will come and make our dwelling with him" (Jn 14:23). This is the "inner" person loved by the Father, loved because he or she has loved much! Is love not possibly what is most needed in our twentieth century, at its beginning, as well as at its end? Is it perhaps not true that the only thing that lasts, without ever losing its validity, is the fact that a person "has loved"?

8. He left this world rather young, but he made a mark upon our entire century, and not only on our century. He left this world, but in the Easter power of his Baptism, he can say to everyone, especially to the young generations of today and tomorrow: "You will see me, because I live and you will live" (Jn 14:19). These words were spoken by Jesus Christ when he took leave of his Apostles before undergoing his Passion. I like to think of them as forming on the lips of our new Blessed himself as a persuasive invitation to live from Christ and in Christ. This invitation is still valid, it is valid today as well, especially for today's young people, valid for everyone. It is a valid invitation which Pier Giorgio Frassati has left for us. Amen.

Cogne, Italy, August 21, 1994

This enchanting place has retained the memory of a young
believer of our century, Pier Giorgio Frassati, whom I had
the joy to proclaim "Blessed" on May 20, 1990. He would
often visit this little town of Cogne. He daringly explored
the peaks towering over it and made each of his ascents an
itinerary to accompany his ascetic and spiritual journey, a
school of prayer and worship, a commitment to discipline
and elevation. He confided to his friends, "Every day that
passes, I fall more desperately in love with the mountains."
And he continued: "I am ever more determined to climb the
mountains, to scale the mighty peaks, to feel that pure joy
which can only be felt in the mountains."

Blessed Pier Giorgio could combine his admiration for the
harmony of creation with his generous service to the Lord
and to his brothers and sisters.

Admiration of creation, admiration of God's work is so
necessary. And may this virtual contemporary of ours, Pier
Giorgio, be an example to all those who go to the mountains. . . . Facing such an extraordinary display of nature, it
comes spontaneously to us to raise our hearts to heaven, just
as young Frassati loved to do frequently.

English editions of *L'Osservatore Romano* containing homilies in which
Pope John Paul II speaks about Pier Giorgio:

April 28, 1980, p. 8.
April 5, 1983, p. 12.
April 24, 1984, p. 24.
July 24, 1989 (no. 30), p. 11.
July 31, 1989 (no. 31), p. 7.
May 20, 1990, Beatification: no. 22 (May 28, 1990).
August 31, 1994 (no. 35), p. 3.

For more information about Pier Giorgio Frassati, contact

Associazione Pier Giorgio Frassati
Via Anicia 12
00153 Rome
Italy

E-mail: mc9018@mclink.it
Website: www.webcom.com/frassati/welcome.html